COLLEEN
McCULLOUGH

COLLEEN McCULLOUGH

A Critical Companion

Mary Jean DeMarr

CRITICAL COMPANIONS TO POPULAR CONTEMPORARY WRITERS
Kathleen Gregory Klein, Series Editor

Greenwood Press
Westport, Connecticut • London

Library of Congress Cataloging-in-Publication Data

DeMarr, Mary Jean.
    Colleen McCullough : a critical companion / Mary Jean DeMarr.
        p.   cm.—(Critical companions to popular contemporary
    writers, ISSN 1082–4979)
    Includes bibliographical references and index.
    ISBN 0–313–29499–2 (alk. paper)
    1.   McCullough, Colleen, 1937–   —Criticism and interpretation.
    2.   Women and literature—Australia—History—20th century.
    I. Title.   II.   Series.
    PR9619.3.M32Z63   1996
    823—dc20   95–50452

British Library Cataloguing in Publication Data is available.

Library of Congress Catalog Card Number: 95–50452
ISBN: 0–313–29499–2
ISSN: 1082–4979

First published in 1996

Greenwood Press, 88 Post Road West, Westport, CT 06881
An imprint of Greenwood Publishing Group, Inc.

Printed in the United States of America

The paper used in this book complies with the
Permanent Paper Standard issued by the National
Information Standards Organization (Z39.48–1984).

10 9 8 7 6 5 4 3 2 1

To Jane, Gene and Rosemary, Paula, and Sharon, with loving thanks for true friendship.

Contents

Series Foreword

The authors who appear in the series Critical Companions to Popular Contemporary Writers are all best-selling writers. They do not have only one successful novel, but a string of them. Fans, critics, and specialist readers eagerly anticipate their next book. For some, high cash advances and breakthrough sales figures are automatic; movie deals often follow. Some writers become household names, recognized by almost everyone.

But novels are read one by one. Each reader chooses to start and, more importantly, to finish a book because of what she or he finds there. The real test of a novel is in the satisfaction its readers experience. This series acknowledges the extraordinary involvement of readers and writers in creating a best-seller.

The authors included in this series were chosen by an Advisory Board composed of high school English teachers and high school and public librarians. They ranked a list of best-selling writers according to their popularity among different groups of readers. Writers in the top-ranked group who had not received book-length, academic literary analysis (or none in at least the past ten years) were chosen for the series. Because of this selection method, Critical Companions to Popular Contemporary Writers meets a need that is not addressed elsewhere.

The volumes in the series are written by scholars with particular expertise in analyzing popular fiction. These specialists add an academic focus to the popular success that these best-selling writers already enjoy.

The series is designed to appeal to a wide range of readers. The general reading public will find explanations for the appeal of these well-known writers. Fans will find biographical and fictional questions answered. Students will find literary analysis, discussions of fictional genres, carefully organized introductions to new ways of reading the novels, and bibliographies for additional research. Students will also be able to apply what they have learned from this book to their readings of future novels by these best-selling writers.

Each volume begins with a biographical chapter drawing on published information, autobiographies or memoirs, prior interviews, and, in some cases, interviews given especially for this series. A chapter on literary history and genres describes how the author's work fits into a larger literary context. The following chapters analyze the writer's most important, most popular, and most recent novels in detail. Each chapter focuses on a single novel. This approach, suggested by the Advisory Board as the most useful to student research, allows for an in-depth analysis of the writer's fiction. Close and careful readings with numerous examples show readers exactly how the novels work. These chapters are organized around three central elements: plot development (how the story line moves forward), character development (what the reader knows about the important figures), and theme (the significant ideas of the novel). Chapters may also include sections on generic conventions (how the novel is similar to or different from others in its same category of science fiction, fantasy, thriller, etc.), narrative point of view (who tells the story and how), symbols and literary language, and historical or social context. Each chapter ends with an "alternative reading" of the novel. The volume concludes with a primary and secondary bibliography, including reviews.

The Alternative Readings are a unique feature of this series. By demonstrating a particular way of reading each novel, they provide a clear example of how a specific perspective can reveal important aspects of the book. In each alternative reading section, one contemporary literary theory—such as feminist criticism, Marxism, new historicism, deconstruction, or Jungian psychological critique—is defined in brief, easily comprehensible language. That definition is then applied to the novel to highlight specific features that might go unnoticed or be understood differently in a more general reading of the novel. Each volume defines two or three specific theories, making them part of the reader's understanding of how diverse meanings may be constructed from a single novel.

Taken collectively, the volumes in the Critical Companions to Popular Contemporary Writers series provide a wide-ranging investigation of the complexities of current best-selling fiction. By treating these novels seriously as both literary works and publishing successes, the series demonstrates the potential of popular literature in contemporary culture.

Kathleen Gregory Klein
Southern Connecticut State University

Acknowledgments

My deepest thanks go to Sharon Anderson, for help with library research; to Kathy Klein, for involving me in this project and encouraging me and patiently answering questions; and to Barbara Rader, for thoughtful help and editing.

1

Colleen McCullough:
The Woman and The Writer

Colleen McCullough seems always to impress those who meet her by her physical appearance and by her presence. Her size—five feet 10 inches and around 200 pounds—her red hair, her chain smoking, her loose-fitting and unfeminine attire, her hearty laugh, and her open personality are regularly commented upon. She accepts comments about her appearance with good grace, telling an interviewer for *People,* a popular gossip magazine, ''I may be big, but at least I have a waistline and a good pair of knockers'' (Fremont-Smith 93). She talks easily and fluently about her writing and is known for gladly meeting with interviewers and readers. She is accessible to her public because accessibility helps her sell books and, it would seem, because she genuinely enjoys talking about her writing. She is a woman of many interests, among them such dissimilar activities as gardening, astronomy, architecture, classical music, cooking (which helped lead her to her first agent, as we will see later), and design and drawing (which she has used in her Roman novels).

PERSONAL DETAILS

Though she is usually thought of as an Australian writer, she has lived most of her adult life outside that country and, in fact, has made it a primary setting for only a few of her novels, including of course *The*

Thorn Birds, the novel that created her reputation. She has written for an American and then an international reading public rather than for the Australia of her own background. She was born on June 1, 1937, in the Australian outback, at Wellington, New South Wales, into a family which moved about a great deal. At various times, she lived in areas of wheat growing, sheep raising, and sugar growing, from which came observations and experiences she later put to use in her fiction, especially in *The Thorn Birds.* She has claimed to be the only bookish person in an athletic family, with a mother who was still climbing mountains at the age of seventy-four. From childhood she has been a voracious reader, claiming to have read around two romances a day during her adolescence and then adding science fiction and adventure to her reading diet.

Sydney eventually became her family's home, and McCullough was educated at Holy Cross College and at the University of Sydney. In high school she excelled in science; when she reached the university level she read widely in the humanities, especially in Roman history. This was the beginning of the interest that would culminate many years later in her Roman novels. However, being born into and influenced by the Great Depression, she turned to science for practical reasons. A job seemed more important than pleasure. At first she hoped to go into medicine, but she was allergic to soap, and since she could not scrub for surgery, she could not train to become a surgeon. As a result, she studied neurophysiology and earned her living for a number of years as a researcher in that field, having previously worked as a teacher in the Outback, as a librarian, and as a journalist. She lived first in England for about four years and then in the United States from 1967 until 1976, where she worked as a research assistant at Yale University in the Department of Neurology in the School of Internal Medicine (she arrived at New Haven on April Fools' Day, 1967!).

Though she had written for herself since childhood, she began writing seriously only during her time at Yale, when she composed her first two novels, *Tim* and *The Thorn Birds,* at night. She had always considered that writing for publication would be a kind of prostitution, but practical considerations eventually made her change her mind. She enjoyed her scientific work, but it did not pay well, and the writing appeared to be a way of earning additional and much needed money. *Tim,* for which she received $50,000, enabled her to pay debts left behind by her father at his death. The success she achieved with her second novel, *The Thorn Birds,* was stunning. It enabled her to give up her scientific employment and live on her own terms. Not long before *The Thorn Birds* was published, but when it was clear that the novel would make a great deal of money, she left Yale and went to England to train as a nurse at St. Bartholemew's Hospital in London. She quickly discovered, however, that the fame she was acquiring as author of a blockbuster success of a novel made it impossible for her to fade into the background as an ordinary nurse trainee. The idea of a rich author carrying bedpans simply seemed ridiculous. She had hoped that from this training would come the background necessary for the hospital novel she then intended to write.

The fame which came along with money from the success of *The Thorn Birds* caused her to make great changes in her life. After building a house in Connecticut and discovering that even there she was subject to pestering by her loyal readers, she sought and found a retreat in the South Pacific. Eventually she settled on Norfolk Island, which is about a thousand miles east of her native Australia. There she can live quietly and write without being constantly interrupted. Norfolk is a green volcanic island with a temperate climate and a small population, which includes descendants of mutineers from the H.M.S. *Bounty*, long ago resettled there from their earlier home on Pitcairn Island. The island is an idyllic setting, with high cliffs, coral reefs, and beautiful beaches.

In her Pacific paradise, McCullough has found a small and congenial community and the isolation she values in order to work. There she has been able to escape the constant attention of press and fans. Eventually the island brought her romantic happiness similar to the kind of happy ending she usually denies her fictional heroines. The differences in age and background between lovers, however, is of the sort she might employ in fiction and seems vaguely reminiscent of the plot of *Tim*. On April 13, 1984, at the age of forty-six, she married Ric Robinson, aged thirty-three, a former housepainter and later a planter, who is descended from a *Bounty* mutineer.

Many details from her own life and observation have appeared in her fiction. Her first two novels and *The Ladies of Missalonghi* rely upon settings from her youth. Her father was a cutter of sugar cane, like Luke in *The Thorn Birds*. Her mother's background as a New Zealander, of partly Maori ancestry, is similar to that of Fee in the same novel. Dane's death by drowning, also in *The Thorn Birds*, reflects the death of McCullough's own brother. A vulgar joke played on Tim in the opening pages of the novel named for him came from McCullough's personal observation. In most of her later work, however, she has turned to settings and materials quite different from those of her Australian background. She has said that she needs to achieve distance from her materials in order to write about them. About ten years away from a place is what she generally requires, though some of the material in her first two novels was twice that old when she finally used it.

From the time of her settling on Norfolk Island and then also from her marriage, her biography has been the story of her professional career as a writer of novels in a variety of genres. Living simply and concentrating on her work, her life has become placid and largely uneventful.

PROFESSIONAL CAREER

The writing histories of *Tim* and *The Thorn Birds* are intertwined. *The Thorn Birds* had long been in her head, but she believed that, as an unknown writer, she would have little chance of finding a publisher for a novel of the length of that family saga. So she wrote *Tim*, intentionally a short and relatively uncomplicated novel, in hopes of establishing herself with it. Thus these first two novels might be called potboilers, in that they were written with practical considerations. The goal was to find a public, to sell books, and to make money. With this achieved, she was able to write more to please herself, and she has said that she no longer likes those first two novels very much. She is particularly hard on *Tim*, which she scorns for the "purple prose" which she later learned to edit out of her writing. In fact, *Tim* is the novel she is least pleased with in retrospect, having even referred to it as "an icky book" (Cassill 32).

It was, however, instrumental in getting her career as a writer started. When *Tim* was finished, she first tried on her own to find a publisher, sending the manuscript out unsolicited and repeatedly receiving it back unread. She realized she would have to find an agent, a professional known to publishers who would, for a percentage of her income on it, attempt to sell it. But she had no better idea of how to find an agent than she did of how to find a publisher. She has later delighted in telling the story of the tuna fish cake and the agent. She was creating a birthday treat for a friend on a tuna fish diet when the manuscript came back yet again. The cake, made with tuna stewed in white wine and molded in a Jello pan in the shape of a fish, was sitting on a table when coincidentally her eye fell on a list of agents and specifically on the name of Frieda Fishbein, whose last name means "fishbone." Taking this as some sort of omen, she "wrote the world's most persuasive letter" (Cassill 34) and sent it to Ms. Fishbein. The latter was amused by the letter and asked to see the manuscript. She liked the book but was not encouraging because of the unconventional heroine and hero (middle-aged spinster and retarded young man) and the Australian setting, unfamiliar to an American reading public. However, she took on the assignment and sold the novel to Harper & Row, which remained McCullough's publisher through her next four novels.

Tim achieved what McCullough had hoped for it: money. Issued in 1974, it sold over 10,000 copies in hardcover and made her over $50,000, a rather unusual success for a first novel. It was filmed in 1981, after the success of *The Thorn Birds* made McCullough's name a powerful draw, with Piper Laurie as Mary Horton and a young Mel Gibson in the title role. The movie is still available in video, and the video cover points out that it is "Based On A Novel By The Author Of "The Thornbirds" [*sic*]," a reminder that any lasting success for this novel relates to the far greater fame of its successor. Avon, her paperback publisher, in fact, did not issue *Tim* in paperback until 1990.

Whatever success *Tim* achieved was far surpassed by *The Thorn Birds,* and McCullough cultivated that success very carefully. The scientific approach learned for her work in neurophysiology applied also, she discovered, to becoming a successful novelist. She went about it methodically, questioning some of her coworkers about what it was in Eric Segal's *Love Story,* a current best-seller, that they liked and what they looked for in a novel. Though like them she was an eager reader of romances, she thought that Segal's novel was "bloody awful." Their answers suggested the characteristics she sought to include in *The Thorn Birds:* ordinary people, not the rich and famous, as characters; humor as an important ingredient; and most important, scenes which move readers to cry. These criteria reminded her of novels such as *East Lynne, Anne of Green Gables,* and *Little Women,* all phenomenally successful. Beth's death scene in *Little Women* seemed a particularly good example of the pull of pathos. She resolved then that her books would always have "buckets of tears" (Cassill 32).

McCullough's reliance on the requirements of these romance readers paid off in the great success achieved by *The Thorn Birds.* Reviewers remarked on the suffering of the strong women, which forms a major part of the novel, as they tried to account for the appeal of the novel. A number of those reviewers confessed themselves engrossed by the story and characters and puzzled by what it was that so held them, much as McCullough had been puzzled by the appeal of *Love Story.* Their conclusions, as well as their reasons for not admiring the novel, varied. If there was a consensus, it was that McCullough could tell a good story and make her readers care about her characters, even if those characters did sometimes seem flat or stereotyped. Critics disagreed over McCullough's use of settings; some found that a great strength of the novel, but one criticized her tendency to separate passage of description from the action of the book.

McCullough was still relatively unknown when *The Thorn Birds* was published in 1977; only *Tim* had preceded it with little critical attention and without wide sales. However, the prepublication excitement over *The Thorn Birds* was extraordinary. Editors and other officials at Harper & Row were so moved by the book and so impressed by its sales potential that they doubled the first printing to 100,000 copies, a very large first run. Stories were told of Harper & Row staff members reading through their tears and staying up all night to finish their prepublication copies. It was a main selection for the Literary Guild and led the best-sellers' lists for six months. Paperback rights were sold at auction and competed for by eight publishers; the finalists were Avon and Bantam, two of the largest mass-market distributors of paperback books. Avon, the winner, paid 1.9 million dollars, then a record (previously held by the 1.85 million dollars paid in 1975 by Bantam for E. L. Doctorow's *Ragtime*). Reportedly, McCullough was to receive half of that amount.

All this furor stimulated a discussion about current publishing trends, which was carried on in magazines interested in the trade. Many knowledgeable critics questioned the increasing concern of publishers for the amount of money which might be made on a particular book, like *The Thorn Birds,* which accompanied, so they thought, a lessening commitment to the quality of books accepted for publication. When publishers are so eager for a blockbuster which will sell millions of copies and make millions of dollars, it was argued, they will concentrate their energies on those popular works, and truly good books which cannot be expected to reach large audiences will find it much more difficult to be published at all (for one discussion of these issues, see Fremont-Smith). McCullough did not participate in this discussion which she had unintentionally inspired, but she has remarked on her belief that quality will ultimately be decided by how well a book lasts: Furthermore, despite her rapid and apparently easy original composition, she repeatedly revises, which suggests her concern for achieving in her writing the highest quality possible.

After its initial publication frenzy, *The Thorn Birds* continued to sell well, indicating its strong appeal to a mass female audience. The showing of a television miniseries, which became a major event in 1983, renewed its sales and created a new controversy. The miniseries, starring Richard Chamberlain as Ralph and Rachel Ward as Meggie, began airing on Palm Sunday, causing protests from the Roman Catholic hierarchy. Several following episodes were broadcast on Passover Seder nights, sacred evenings for many Jewish viewers, making the religious protests seem interfaith. The United States Catholic Conference called the scheduling an "affront to good taste and religious sensibilities" (Prial 48). The Conference's objection was primarily to the sympathetic portrayal of a Roman Catholic priest who breaks his vows, particularly offensive in view of the sensationally sexual nature of that disobedience. ABC, the network on which the series was shown, indicated that the scheduling had been necessary because constraints caused by the occurrence of other events which the network was committed to cover left only the Holy Week and Passover time slots available. McCullough played no part in this controversy, which indicates the sensitivity of some of the material in her novel and thus in its television translation, as well as the appeal expected for— and achieved by—the series based on her work. Sales of the novel had reached 675,000 copies in hardcover and 11 million in paperback by 1989, and it continues to sell steadily in paperback to the present.

The great—if controversial—success of *The Thorn Birds* freed McCullough to become a full-time professional author and to live as she wished, leading to her eventual settling on Norfolk Island. Later novels have been more original than *Tim* and *The Thorn Birds*, in which she felt forced by the requirements of the mass market to conform to some extent to the dictates of public taste. Subsequent books have also been less successful, when judged by sales and profits.

An Indecent Obsession, McCullough's first novel after *The Thorn Birds* and published four years later in 1981, profited from the expectations raised by the runaway success of its predecessor. Before publication, it had four printings with 200,000 copies. By 1989 it had sold 323,000 copies in hardcover and 2.6 million in paperback. Those figures are notably below the equivalent figures for *The Thorn Birds* but still quite respectable. It is her first novel set outside her native Australia but uses Australian characters. In making use of a hospital setting, even though a military hospital with its special characteristics, *An Indecent Obsession*, like her earlier books, relies on her own background. It also continues to make use of some of the romance elements that have underlain both *Tim* and *The Thorn Birds*, though those elements are less important than are other structural elements. *An Indecent Obsession*, as a straight novel with psychological themes, seems aimed at a general public interested in novels of ideas rather than at a female audience seeking an evocation of their fantasies. The most obvious market for her fiction has thus been altered and it has shrunk.

Where *The Thorn Birds* had puzzled and dismayed some reviewers, who found themselves trying with difficulty to account for its appeal despite what they saw as its flaws, reviewers of *An Indecent Obsession* tended to comment on its differences from the earlier book and to praise it by comparison. In turning away from fiction, which could be easily dismissed as "formula" writing, McCullough won some respect at the cost of a wide readership and financial gains. She observed later, about her Roman novels, that while she does not care particularly about money, she cares deeply about her work. It might be pointed out that the freedom from debt brought her by *Tim* and the far greater freedom from other pressures brought by *The Thorn Birds* enabled her to take this idealistic position. In any event, from *An Indecent Obsession* on, her work has clearly been what she wanted it to be, not what she thought a mass market wanted. Nevertheless, she has continued to be accessible to her public during extensive publicity tours on the occasion of newly published novels, and she has been open and welcoming to interviewers.

An Indecent Obsession reveals McCullough's new freedom to take her work seriously for its own sake principally in being concerned with theme more than the earlier books had been. Here, instead of creating characters to tell a story or to involve the fantasies of readers, she has seemed to create characters and a story in order to examine certain ideas about duty, responsibility, guilt, and how people relate to each other. In this regard, then, *An Indecent Obsession* is a more serious novel than its predecessors. Reviewers noted this deeper seriousness with mixed reactions. Some felt the novel became too plodding, too obviously driven by ideas, and thus was not very compelling as a story. Christopher Lehmann-Haupt in the *New York Times,* however, even while suggesting that the story and characters were on the level of soap opera, thought that the improvement over *The Thorn Birds* was substantial enough to warrant beginning to take her seriously as a novelist (C24).

With her next book, McCullough turned in a surprising direction. She continued her interest in the fiction of ideas, but now she turned completely away from her Australian settings and characters and tried her hand at a genre entirely new to her. Even more obviously than *An Indecent Obsession, A Creed for the Third Millennium*, published in 1985, is a novel of ideas. A serious use of science fiction—more exactly, of the dystopia—it predicts what life might be like in the first third of the twenty-first century in order to suggest some solutions for social problems and attitudes existing in the present. By 1989 it had sold 83,000 copies in hardback and 1.75 million in paperback, decidedly fewer even than *An Indecent Obsession*. Reviewers were not kind to McCullough's experimentation with a new form, pointing out examples of triteness, of unexplained elements in her basic situation, and of too obvious parallels between her characters and plot and the story of Jesus Christ and early Christianity on which they are based. Her seriousness of intent was not doubted, but the quality of her book was. Clearly, McCullough was writing with purpose here, and some reviewers did note that the message of the novel had meaning and relevance for readers concerned about prevailing moods and attitudes in the 1980s. That this novel remains in print seems largely due to the continuing pull of McCullough's name— had it been written by an unknown author it seems doubtful it would continue to be available, a statement that could also be made for *Tim* and the novel which followed this one, *The Ladies of Missalonghi*.

A novelette rather than a novel, *The Ladies of Missalonghi*, published in 1987, returns to McCullough's Australian setting and characters and to the romance form. It was one of a series of short books published in Harper's Short Novel Series and had a first printing of 100,000 copies, partly no doubt because of the reputation of its author. Its sales by 1989 in hardcover were 117,000 and in paperback 1.5 million. Hardcover sales were larger than those for *A Creed for the Third Millennium* but paperback sales were down. Two reasons would seem obvious for the increase in hardcover sales: the inclusion of the novelette in a series of books and its apparent appeal as a romance. The continuing drop in paperback sales is perhaps the clearest evidence of McCullough's loss of the mass market she had achieved with *The Thorn Birds*. Like *The Thorn Birds, The Ladies of Missalonghi* embroiled her in controversy when it was pointed out that her novelette was closely patterned after a forgotten novel by L. M. Montgomery, whose better known *Anne of Green Gables* is one of the sentimental novels she had listed as an example of the uses of tears in women's fiction. That controversy, however, was fought in the New Zealand and Australian press and had little if any effect on McCullough's reputation in the United States. It should also be pointed out that this novel had its own success as a Reader's Digest Condensed Books selection and an alternate selection of the Literary Guild. *The Ladies of Missalonghi* is a minor book, a brief interlude in her career.

With *The First Man in Rome* she began her most ambitious project to date, and with the series of Roman novels she has turned herself into a historical novelist concerned with accuracy of detail rather than with giving her readers frequent opportunities to weep. With these novels she has begun a work of which she is proud and of whose quality she is protective. Indicating why she has chosen to write historical fiction rather than straight history, she has commented that it is fiction, not nonfiction, which endures and that since she has no children, her books are her gift to the future, her attempt at immortality. Her concern for the quality of what she writes and her hope that it will endure are obvious.

The Roman novels are a projected series of five thoroughly researched books based on the fall of the Roman republic and focusing on—or leading up to—the life and career of Julius Caesar. The first of these books, *The First Man in Rome,* appeared in 1990, and succeeding novels were intended to appear each year until the series was complete. However, it is not surprising, given the length and complexity of these novels, that their appearance has been slower than originally announced. *The Grass Crown* was published in 1991, *Fortune's Favorites* in 1993, and *Caesar's Women* in 1996. These are exceedingly ambitious undertakings, each based on thorough research and requiring careful construction, for they interweave the stories of many actual historical figures into a fabric which is quite varied.

Their publication history began with something of a furor, when it was learned that McCullough, associated with Harper & Row for her entire career, was moving to another publisher. Harper & Row was perhaps understandably hesitant about undertaking to publish a series of five lengthy novels about a period of history not especially known for its fascination to the American reading public. Not only that, but this subject was entirely new to the fiction of this particular novelist, whose greatest triumph for them had, after all, been some years earlier with *The Thorn Birds* and had been followed by a varied collection of novels of generally decreasing sales and public notice. Nevertheless, Harper & Row expressed some anger at her desertion of their house, which had stuck by her despite those lessening profits. The publishing house issued a statement in which it accused McCullough, by implication, of bargaining in bad faith for publishing rights to these novels. "We had negotiated a deal, and had Colleen's verbal agreement to publish these novels for a royalty advance for $3 million for world rights," the statement reads. "However, Colleen apparently had a change of heart, and instructed her agent . . . to make a deal with Morrow and Avon. . . . We were presented with a *fait accompli* which is particularly distressing given our long relationship" (Feldman 40).

McCullough's version of the events leading up to her change of publishers is, not unexpectedly, quite different. She felt that Harper & Row was not according her and her work the respect she and it had earned. There was a disagreement about the size and structure of the series, with McCullough definitely anticipating five novels and the eventual possibility of seven, while Harper & Row insisted that it be limited to three novels. This limitation was unacceptable to McCullough, who thought it would damage her concept of the project into which she had already poured so much work and saw it as a loss of faith in her work on the part of her longtime publisher. As negotiations proceeded, she came more and more to believe that the publishing house's resistance to accepting her project as she envisioned it meant a "lack of confidence" (Feldman 40).

At Morrow, the Roman novels were well received; the first novel had a prepublication printing of 300,000. It was also a selection of the Book-of-the-Month Club, ensuring broad general sales. Reviewers of all three novels have often mentioned *The Thorn Birds* (but not the other novels) as a way of identifying the author and have not infrequently noted how different this later project is from her most famous work. They have commented on the great amount of research going into the novels but have disagreed on the quality of the fiction resulting. One reviewer, for instance, called *The First Man in Rome* "airport fiction at its best" (*Time* 15 October 1990: 88), and another evaluated *The Grass Crown* as "a quietly magnificent tour de force" (*Publishers Weekly* 9 August 1991: 43). Another reviewer, on the other hand, mocked her style in *The Grass Crown* and summed it all up as "Hopefully, off-putting" (Jennings 13). Reviews in general were favorable, praising McCullough's recreation of a past age which is little known to most readers and her imaginative combination of historical materials with compelling characters and dramatic action.

The subject of these novels is one that had interested McCullough since her college years, when she began reading classical Roman writers. She is said to have had dreams of writing these books for some thirty years, and she had worked on the research for them for approximately ten years before she began to write. She found a great thrill in reading the actual words of ancient figures who had made history, not just written about it, and she acquired a large and fine private library on the subject of Republican Rome, one which she claims is the best in the world. For her, writers like Cicero and Julius Caesar created "a world that I wanted to enter as a novelist, desperately" (Steinberg 109). Ironically, of course, her excitement at reading the actual words of Caesar and Cicero inspired her to become yet another of those writers "scribbling away after the fact" (Steinberg 109). Her decision to write fiction, not history, however, surely relates not just to the fact that she is a novelist and not a trained historian. Even more basic is her desire to convey the world, the excitement she felt at entering their consciousness while reading their words, not just the desire to struggle with their ideas and to figure out what happened and when it took place.

The variety of McCullough's fiction, resulting from her refusal to fit herself into any one genre or approach has so far kept her fresh. Each new project, whatever its strengths and weaknesses, has the virtue of originality and freshness. She once observed that she had in mind a number of novels of varying types, hoping "to have a bash at every genre" (Reuter 27). What she will do when the immense Roman project is finished is impossible to predict.

WRITING METHODS

About McCullough's writing methods, a few main comments are particularly obvious and have often been pointed out. These refer to the speed with which she composes, the care and pains with which she revises, and the thoroughness of her research. Her speed of composition was particularly frequently noted early in her career, especially in regard to *The Thorn Birds,* which she wrote in marathon sessions during her free time while holding down a full-time job as a scientific researcher at Yale. She sometimes wrote for sixteen hours straight and then refreshed herself by napping. She can maintain this concentration of effort perhaps because of the long planning that often occurs before writing begins. Books may be in her head for years before she actually begins to write them. *The Thorn Birds*, in fact, was pretty much mentally written before she began to write *Tim,* though the latter, a shorter and simpler novel, was published first. The much later Roman novels were a dream for some thirty years and were under research for ten years before their actual writing began.

Although the writing often proceeds with great rapidity, it is followed by meticulous revision. Novels go through many drafts as McCullough tries to ensure that they meet her standards. Her earliest drafts, written at great speed, tend to be her shortest, with succeeding drafts increasing in length. Stories are told of her work on *The Thorn Birds,* which included stints of fifteen thousand words in a night, typing about eighty words a minute. The record is said to be a single session in which she produced thirty thousand words. As a result of the hard physical effort required for these writing sessions, her legs swelled and her fingers blistered, so that she took to wearing gloves for typing. Original drafts would seem to be the pouring out onto the page of the materials that have been seething in her head, often for years; revision and editing are required to clarify and smooth this mass of material. Tales which emphasize the speed of her composition, she says, both exaggerate her prowess and underestimate her craft. Long books especially require a great deal of revision; her reworking of *The Thorn Birds* entailed much rearrangement and expansion of what had been in the earliest drafts.

She tends to add and amplify rather than cut as she revises and edits. She does, she says, sometimes cut passages where the style displeases her. It is the presence of that overwriting in *Tim* that explains, partly at least, her particular dislike of her first novel. She may have written the initial two drafts of *The Thorn Birds* quickly, but the process of revising— those eight additional drafts—continued for many months. Similarly, *An Indecent Obsession* went through thirteen drafts, occupying seven months in which she often worked as much as fourteen hours a day. Clearly, the process of writing and revising for McCullough becomes almost obsessive.

McCullough believes in doing all her own work. She pointed out, at the time of the publication of *The Thorn Birds,* that she did all her own typing and all her own research. She does not believe in employing anyone else to do research for her, and she claims to be a particularly skilled typist. A sidelight on the frenzied writing of the early books is that she acquired a collection of typewriters, which she called by nicknames, such as "Prince," "Rex," "Spot," and "Rover" (Cassill 34), humorous names suggesting that she thought of them almost as pets! (She also names her houseplants.) She is insistent on certain stylistic usages, arguing with copy editors who made changes that she thought harmed her rhythms. The absence of a comma in the opening paragraph of *The Thorn Birds,* removed by a copy editor and overlooked by her, is damaging to the paragraph in her view. And she insists on the British spellings of "axe" and "grey" because they seem more axelike and greyer (Cassill 35).

One type of writing that she has mentioned finding particularly difficult is love scenes, particularly scenes with sexual content. *The Thorn Birds* is notable for containing little explicit sex, unlike many contemporary novels in the family saga or historical romance genres, perhaps because of her distaste for this sort of scene as it is often written and her perception that such activities are more effectively suggested than explicitly described. The emotion, not the mechanics of the sex act, is what she finds interesting and what she attempts to convey. But at the same time, she is intent on communicating the erotic content as well as the feelings. As a result, love scenes may go through a particularly high number of drafts, up to sixty she has claimed.

McCullough's craft was no less meticulous in her process of creating the Roman series. The difference in these novels was the need for research into the biographies of historical figures and background about events and everyday life of the period of the late Roman republic. She believes that her training as a scientist helps her, since she is used to doing research. For this excursion into the ancient world, she amassed a library and immersed herself in it. This time, however, she relented on one of her principles and hired a researcher, with fluency in several languages, who interviewed a number of international experts in the field. When she had her mounds of research, she began writing—but not yet for the novels. She wrote long essays on her major characters and constructed a detailed chronology of events. This preparatory writing was completed for the entire series before she began to draft the opening novel and before she began to dicker with Harper & Row about publishing the project. The fact that she had already poured such great effort into it explains why she was insistent, to the point of breaking off a long-standing relationship with her original publisher, that her plan for the entire series be followed.

The kind of attention to detail that she prides herself upon, and which helps explain her habit of repeated revision, is particularly obvious in the Roman novels. They are extremely long, around eight hundred pages each. That length she defends, saying that she has "only one maxim: a book should be as long as it has to be, not one word more, not one word less" (McCullough, "Reflections" 1). The excitement of the little discoveries made while doing research is important to her, and she uses those little discoveries to bring life to her historical materials. She calls herself a "nitpicker" who loves the "little details," which to her are what "make[s] it sing," what "makes the world very real" (Steinberg 110). She has also described the moment of discovery as being "as real and as heartlifting between the pages of Pliny the Elder as it is in gazing upon the sources of the Nile," giving one the "conviction that one has peeled back a frontier, even if the frontier is no more than inside one's own mind" (McCullough, "Reflections" 3).

The progress of McCullough's career as a writer from romantic novelist (even if a critical user of that genre) to serious historical novelist reveals a woman with tremendous gusto for her work and sincere dedication to her craft. That she is not taken more seriously as a novelist probably results partly from the fact that she began with enormous popular success in genres not much respected by academic critics. Like Hollywood starlets attempting to switch from being sex goddesses to serious actresses, novelists find it difficult to be accepted as serious writers after earlier commercial and popular successes. Her continued popularity with a wide public has been hindered by her switching from genre to genre, so that a fan of one novel will not necessarily have any interest in her other work. And yet her novels, not just *The Thorn Birds,* find their readers. McCullough writes of receiving "enormous amounts of mail from readers of the Roman novels," the books which have achieved the greatest critical admiration and would seem, because of their length and masses of detail, to be least appealing to the popular taste. Though she has stepped back from her early and very conscious attempts to make money from her writing, she continues to promote her books energetically, making publication tours for her publishers and giving interviews generously. But most important, she is now writing what she wants to write, for a publisher which issues it in the length and form she dictates. The fruits of her success have been the power to live and write as she wishes, and she has taken full advantage of that success.

2

A Writer of Many Genres

When the name of Colleen McCullough is mentioned, most readers immediately think of the genres (or types of novels) of romance and family saga. This association comes from her single greatest success, *The Thorn Birds,* which does indeed fit into those categories. But this novel is far from typical of her work. Indeed, there is no such thing as a typical McCullough novel. This author refuses to write to any formula and challenges herself to do something new and different with each new project she undertakes. She writes what have often been described as old-fashioned novels, straightforward in the telling and concentrating on such themes as love, duty, responsibility, revenge, and the like. So far she has published eight novels, which fall into six different patterns. The number of patterns is less than the number of novels simply because the last three books are the first part of a connected series, which necessitates that those books resemble each other.

A chronological reminder will be helpful here. The order of publication of McCullough's novels and their genres is as follows:

Tim (1974)—a romance (loosely interpreted)

The Thorn Birds (1977)—a family saga with elements of romance

An Indecent Obsession (1981)—a psychological novel with elements of the mystery

A Creed for the Third Millennium (1985)—a dystopia

The Ladies of Missalonghi (1987)—a romance/antiromance/parody of romance

"The Masters of Rome" series—historical novels:

> *The First Man in Rome* (1990)
>
> *The Grass Crown* (1991)
>
> *Fortune's Favorites* (1993)
>
> *Caesar's Women* (1996).

Two conclusions follow from the above listing. First, a number of the novels do not fit easily into conventional genre categories. And second, the romance genre is the most predominant of the conventional types, having some application to at least three of the eight novels or, to put it another way which makes the importance of romance even clearer, in three of the five projects (considering the historical series as one connected project).

Until the last thirty years, or so, fiction which appealed to a mass market was not taken seriously or studied in schools and colleges. Only what is now thought of as "elite" literature had a real place in the curriculum. The distinction between "popular" and "elite" becomes crucial when we look at the writings of authors who regularly produce bestsellers. These terms are often defined in opposition to each other. Popular literature at one time could be rather simply defined as that literature and those literary types not studied in the schools. Elite literature then included that which was considered respectable enough to have entered the curriculum. Now that popular literature, like popular culture in general, has become an object of study, that handy and simplistic definition no longer works satisfactorily.

A more useful definition distinguishes between what people—or a society—consider they should read and what they actually do read. It is the difference between what is produced for a mass market and what appeals to a select and highly educated public. Popular culture is sometimes related to folklore (and indeed folklore is one aspect of popular culture), in that folklore contains what ordinary, even uneducated, people actually believe and do and say. Popular fiction is what ordinary people actually like to read—and what many intellectuals read in their leisure hours.

Though now rather old and somewhat outdated, John G. Cawelti's important book, *Adventure, Mystery, and Romance: Formula Stories as Art and Popular Culture* (1976), discusses and defines several forms of popular literature and analyzes examples of each. Ironically, despite the title of his study, he does not examine in depth the genre of romance, a type usually associated with female writers and readers. This omission was possible in 1976, when the women's movement was still gaining strength and before the growth of feminist criticism. In fairness, however, it must be admitted that other types, such as science fiction and horror, are also omitted. Cawelti's principal interest is in the formulas or familiar patterns (in plotting and narrative, primarily) which delight readers. He points out that many readers, especially readers who look for escape, "find a special delight in familiar stories," which means not only stories they have already heard but also "certain types of stories which have highly predictable structures that guarantee the fulfillment of conventional expectations: the detective story, the western, the romance, the spy story, and many other such types." He refers to these as "formulaic types" (Cawelti 1). Cawelti seems to define "popular" as types which rely on formulas, and he points out that there is no one mass audience, that most people participate in the popular culture from time to time. Thus though the types of literary works may be distinguished from each other, the audiences cannot so easily be separated.

By "formulas," Cawelti means "narrative and dramatic structures that form such a large part of the cultural diet of the majority of readers, television viewers, and film audiences" (2). These familiar elements let the reader know what to expect—a happy ending, the blissful union of heroine and hero, the solution to a crime, and so on. Knowing in general terms what is to come, the reader is freed to enjoy the events, the story that transports her or him along the way. Bookstores take advantage of these interests of readers by segregating their wares into sections by genre. Mysteries, horror, science fiction, and romance will all usually be found shelved in separate sections, well apart from a general section of "literature." Often enough, however, there is overlap, and it is not clear why a novel is placed in a particular section. A kind of literary and historical snobbery is sometimes involved, so that a novel like Charlotte Brontë's *Jane Eyre*, the single book most influential in establishing the modern romance, will be found in the general literature section rather than in the section for romance.

Some authors find a niche in a particular genre. Building a public which looks for their novels in that genre because of the familiarity and security of having "a good read," whose effects they can predict, ensures that the members of that writer's public will return again and again to the author. While reviewers tend to pay less and less attention to each succeeding book, perhaps because their increased predictability leaves less of interest for the reviewer to say, readers respond in the opposite manner, and publishers will accept the work because it is a sure thing with a preexisting public. Thus the creation of a formula, or the working within an established formula, may enable an author to survive as a writer.

Occasionally a writer who succeeds in a particular genre, however, will refuse to be pigeonholed in that genre. And some authors manipulate the "rules" of particular genres in ways which alter them significantly, sometimes in such a way as to criticize a genre itself. Colleen McCullough has done both those things. She scorns writers who produce what she calls "formula Books" (Rovner C23). Known as a writer of family saga and romance, she has refused to limit herself to those genres, and her uses of those genres are in varying degrees different from those of many other writers.

Examining McCullough's novels in chronological order to try to discover any progression in her choice of genres (that is, particular periods in which she was interested in one genre or another, logical shifts from genre to genre, and so on) leads to few helpful conclusions. Conclusions may be drawn about other elements of her fictional practice such as themes (or ideas) and settings (or the places in which her stories take place). But there seems to be no particular pattern except that of continual experimentation in her choices of genre. Therefore, the genres appearing in her fiction will be examined in a more or less logical order rather than in order of her use of them. First will be the psychological novel, the one genre McCullough uses which is not thought of as a particularly popular type. Then, turning to the popular genres, we will begin with the romance, McCullough's favorite genre and one which underlies several of the other genres in her use of it. Next, since it is closest to the romance in McCullough's practice, we'll examine the family saga. Finally, turning away from the various applications of romance, we will look at the dystopia and the historical novel, two forms that are related to each other in that each is based on a created world which is quite different from that known to the reader.

PSYCHOLOGICAL NOVEL

Of all the genres examined here, this is the one not usually considered a popular genre. The psychological novel may be simply defined as a work of fiction centered around the psychology of one or more of its characters. It may be a psychological study of abnormal behavior, or it may be the depiction of a character who is intensely involved with motivations and choices and whose feelings and thoughts are then examined in detail. This type of fiction has a long and respectable history, appealing to such great writers as Thomas Hardy, Joseph Conrad, and James Joyce.

All fiction, of course, is psychological, in that all fiction relies on character depiction and thus necessitates a realistic examination of the inner states of individuals portrayed. However, some fiction relies most heavily on action for its primary interest, just as other fiction concentrates on psychology. Thus it is a matter of degree, not of kind. When observing the interior life of characters or understanding why they act as they do becomes of crucial interest, we may say that we have a psychological novel. This very broad genre includes novels which are overtly and obviously psychological in that they directly discuss and even analyze the feelings of characters. The fiction of Henry James illustrates this approach. At the other extreme, a novelist like Ernest Hemingway may choose to hint at or indirectly reveal the thoughts and feelings of his characters by describing objectively what they do and say as well as what they observe. In such novels as *The Sun Also Rises* and *A Farewell to Arms,* readers deduce or intuit the feelings of the characters from their behavior and observations.

In all her novels, McCullough is, of course, interested in the psychology of her central characters. Feelings, choices, and motivations are always examined, sometimes at length, and these interior elements are always important to the overall effect of her narratives. However, in *An Indecent Obsession* she has written what is strictly speaking a novel of this genre. Set in a mental ward, this novel, which presents case studies of several unbalanced individuals, centers on the effects of the actions of one man whose mental condition is at issue. Luce seems a sane man misplaced among others who are obviously unhinged. And he is as lucid as his name implies, but his is the lucidity of a psychopath. His portrait is that of a representative of evil, a man who is so self-involved and so filled with malice and anger that he has no hesitation in following the impulses that lead him consciously and intentionally to destroy—or attempt to destroy—others. His manipulativeness, shown in detail, is a part of his clever and deeply abnormal mentality.

An Indecent Obsession carries through its theme of psychological probing in other ways. Luce is not the actual center of the action, but rather the antagonist, one who is in conflict with the true central characters. His behavior enables McCullough to examine the mental states of other characters, who include both unbalanced patients, at least one obviously sane patient, and the nurse who cares for them all. The interactions among these various characters and especially the ways in which the arrival of a new inmate upsets the delicate balance achieved among nurse and patients become a significant interest for the reader. While the novel, as so often in McCullough's work, contains important elements of romance, the love story is thwarted by the psychological needs of the characters and eventually by their moral standards and choices. Understanding and accepting responsibility for their actions is an important outcome.

While *An Indecent Obsession* is easily categorized as a psychological novel, it contains elements often associated with other genres and thus, to some extent, it mixes literary types. The action is not purely interior and relational. The psychological maneuvering of the characters climaxes in a murder. Because the facts of that murder are for some time withheld from the reader, elements of suspense and mystery are important in the latter portions of the novel, relating this book to the genre of mystery fiction. However, after the details of the killing are revealed, the interest of the plot returns to the psychological, specifically to ways in which the knowledge of the fact of murder and the identity of the murderer will affect the lives of those remaining. And so ultimately, despite a certain mixing of methods, the central identification of *An Indecent Obsession* as a psychological novel, McCullough's only clear entry in that category, remains accurate.

ROMANCE

The genre of romance might be considered basic in McCullough's work. Most broadly defined, a romance is a love story. The term has a long and somewhat confusing history, for it was first applied to narrative poems (poetry that tells a story) of the middle ages in which knights rode out to perform heroic deeds. In the process, they often rescued fair maidens, though the love story was not a necessary part of the plot and was always secondary to the questing of the knight. Later, the term came to be applied to longer prose fictions in which action predominated and in which there was some aspect of the wonderful or strange. Again, a love story was often involved, but the reader's main interest was in the adventure of a male protagonist. Sometimes romance simply refers to prose fictions which contain some use of the supernatural or at least those which do not conform to the requirements of the realistic novel that every aspect of a story be absolutely believable by the reader as possible to happen in everyday life. This was the distinction made by Nathaniel Hawthorne between the novel and the romance, considered the romance superior because of its ability to examine psychology and to use symbolism in ways he thought the realistic novel could not.

The word "romance" still carries all of these meanings in literary criticism today. Its meaning in discussion of popular fiction combines something of the more modern literary meanings with its popular denotation. The popular romance today is a genre which appeals primarily to women readers and which centers around a love story. Adventure and suspense as well as exotic settings are often part of the contemporary romance. The mass-marketed romances, under such trade names as "Silhouette" and "Harlequin," tend to rely on conventional notions about female and male roles and to center around stereotyped characters. Male characters are strong, brave, often somewhat mysterious, and with a hint of something ominous in their background. Females are weaker, sometimes naive and apt to rush into situations they do not understand. Their role is to be rescued, while the male's role is either to threaten or to rescue. Perhaps as one effect of the feminist movement, female characters are tending to become stronger and more competent, but the conventional happy ending—the joyous woman in the arms of her powerful lover—is still expected by readers and provided by writers and publishers.

Cawelti calls the romance "perhaps the simplest fantasy archetype" and defines it as the "feminine equivalent of the adventure story" (41). He distinguishes between the adventure story and the romance by pointing out that, in the adventure story, any romance is "distinctly subsidiary to the hero's triumph over dangers and obstacles," while in the romance the reverse is true (41). He summarizes several particular formulaic plots, such as the Cinderella story (poor girl marries rich or powerful man), the Pamela tale (poor girl overcomes dangers of purely physical lust to create a truly meaningful relationship), and the contemporary career girl story (career girl is torn between work and love and finally selects love as the really fulfilling option) (42). In all these—and other—varieties of romance, Cawelti quite rightly points out that the romance formula supports conventional "affirmations of the ideals of monogamous marriage and feminine domesticity" (42). As Bridgwood suggests, the "romantic relationship is the place where women find their authentic selves and have their identities established, completed and confirmed" (167). Fictional romances depict the creation of such relationships, which explains their appeal to audiences of women and their conservative support of traditional gender roles.

With none of these generalizations is McCullough comfortable, though much of her work is closely allied to romance forms. She has read widely in the genre, once observing, "I was weaned on romances" (Rovner C23). Though she is often thought of as a writer of romance, and though her novels contain many plots that might be called "love stories," in none of them does she present the conventional formulaic happy ending of romance. *Tim* turns the genre upside down, depicting a strong woman and a weak and helpless man. In almost every way, they reverse the roles expected of man and woman in a romance. Yet this is one of only two of her novels which conclude with what might be called happy endings, and its conclusion is far from conventional. McCullough's other book which comes close to the genre of romance, *The Ladies of Missalonghi*, written after three major books had intervened, disturbs the expected principles of romance just as strongly as *Tim,* though in a different manner. Here McCullough accepts conventional gender roles but tinkers with plot and character in several crucial ways. She casts doubt on the ethics of her heroine, a decided breaking of readers' expectations, and she creates a literal fairy grandmother (actually a guardian angel) to bring about the happy ending. Thus it is not so much love which conquers all as it is the heroine's unscrupulous behavior and the manipulations from behind the scenes of the hero's dead wife. *The Ladies of Missalonghi* is perhaps a parody of the romance genre or of a particular novel—L.M. Montgomery's *The Blue Castle*—and perhaps a plagiarized version of that novel, which is in fact a good example of a sentimental romance. In either event, *The Ladies of Missalonghi* is better seen as an antiromance than as an exemplar of the romance form.

These two books come at the beginning and near the middle of McCullough's career. Love stories and thus elements of romance appear in all her other books except *A Creed for the Third Millennium*, but none of these other novels is centered around the single love story in the same way. *The Thorn Birds* contains the most romance elements, principally through the long love affair of Meggie and Father Ralph, but theirs is an ill-fated love, doomed to failure from the beginning and thus not a conventional romance. Additionally, in recounting the affairs of three generations of one family, this long novel goes beyond the limits of the typical romance.

McCullough's other novels, *An Indecent Obsession* and the Roman books, contain love stories which are subordinated to other elements. In the former, the romantic elements form only one strand of the psychological studies truly at the center of the novel, and in the latter, a number of very realistic sexual and familial relationships between women and men are portrayed as subplots to what is primarily the story of the lives of Roman men. In neither case are ''happily-ever-after'' romantic endings provided. Thus these books, which now form a large proportion of McCullough's work, can in no way be considered romances. Despite her often being thought of as a teller of love stories, an overview of her career indicates that this is not the case.

FAMILY SAGA

Of all the genres McCullough employs, the family saga is probably used most nearly as readers of the genre would have expected. The genre contains novels, often of great length, which follow the adventures of members of several generations of one family. These novels contain a large number of characters, with entire new casts of dramatic personages created for the new stories of the succeeding generations. Skilled novelists draw parallels between the adventures and experiences of the various groups, showing how the experiences—or the sins—of one generation are influential or even causative on the experiences of those who follow them.

These novels contain elements taken from many other genres. There may be embedded romances or mysteries, for example, and the romance or mystery of one generation may set up conditions which control or at least influence the actions of that generation's daughters and sons. Old enmities may be carried from one generation to another, and loves thwarted in one generation may be fulfilled in the offspring of the first lovers. Paradoxically, the family saga opposes some elements of the romance. As Bridgwood points out, marriage, the goal of the romance novel, ''is never the straightforward means of precipitating the narrative climax and conclusion that it is in romance" (167). Since one generation's story must lead to that of the next, only the final generation can present closure (an ending or conclusion with a final resolution of themes). Of necessity, some part of a multigenerational family saga will be historical, even if its later portions are set in or near the present of the author and readers. What is required for a successful novel of this type is that the stories be connected, and this may be done in a variety of ways—through a continuing character or two, through the paralleling of plots, or through the development of themes from generation to generation. In some ways, then, this genre is freer of specific conventions of plot and character than are many other popular genres, though many such novels rely heavily on adventure and romance.

McCullough's single venture into the family saga, her most successful novel, is typical in a number of ways. It depicts the historical past, the period of World War I in New Zealand and Australia and the following decades. It covers three generations of one family, makes important use of love stories, and ties its various sections together through the continuing presence of several major characters (Fiona, who becomes the matriarch of the family, and Meggie, whose life from childhood to approaching old age gives the novel its span) as well as through parallels in plotting and continuing themes and images. As always, however, McCullough does not simply accept the conventions of the genre she is using. She adapts them, placing her greatest emphasis on the middle of the three generations she covers. In this family saga, interest is not spread relatively evenly over the generations and groups covered. McCullough has structured her novel symmetrically, with the story of the earliest period for the Cleary family shown mainly to lead into the tale of Meggie's and Father Ralph's love and with the story of Justine and Rainer set up as an aftermath and conclusion to the themes and plots which could not be completed in the middle generation. Thus *The Thorn Birds*, while following the major descriptive characteristics of the genre, uses them to suit the needs of McCullough's particular story and characters.

Additionally, it should be pointed out that McCullough's characterization is innovative. Her most central romantic hero, because he is a Roman Catholic priest, cannot possibly be the hero of a conventional romance, and thus insofar as the family saga makes use of romance elements, this novel is unconventional. However, as hero for one section of a family saga his very disqualification—his vow of celibacy—is particularly useful. It motivates the thwarting of his and Meggie's affair and thus leads on to the generation of Meggie's daughter with unresolved passions and themes.

It might be argued that there are elements of family saga in McCullough's Roman novels, since a number of families are followed through several generations there, with the political sins of the fathers often being punished in the generations of the sons. Caesars, Ptolemys, Mariuses, and many other, less prominent, families are depicted in several generations and in their complicated extended families. However, the very fact that these stories are all intermixed so that no one family, not even the Caesars, takes center stage gives these books a very different tone and texture from the usual family saga. Their often brutal realism plus the reader's constant awareness that these are largely the facts of history also removes from them the sense of adventure and romance so typical of books like *The Thorn Birds*.

DYSTOPIA

Dystopias make up a subgenre closely related to or developing from several other sorts of fiction. It is helpful to be reminded that all fiction relies on the creation of imagined worlds. Every novel or short story implies within itself a world which has its own rules and assumptions and operates on its own terms. A writer may use the same world in several works, continuing the use of the same characters and settings, or each new work may suggest its own world. Among those genres in which the creation of imagined worlds is particularly obvious are fantasy and science fiction, for in those types the worlds are recognizably different from the everyday world we all think we inhabit. It should be pointed out, however, that just as the "real" world differs a bit for each of us (as a result of our differing perceptions and experiences, which cause us to see things from our own special perspective), so even the worlds created by apparently "realistic" writers are special to those particular works.

In fantasy, the created world is clearly unrealistic, obviously not the same as the world any reader would recognize from daily life. The setting may be unreal, for example, such as fairyland or some mythical land resembling our most romanticized notions of the chivalric middle ages. The unreality may also be in characters, who might, perhaps, have magical powers. J.R.R. Tolkien's Middle Earth, in his series "The Lord of the

Rings," is a particularly interesting example of fantasy in which an unreal but believable world contains some very realistic and some very unrealistic characters. One of the problems of *The Ladies of Missalonghi*, in fact, is its inclusion of one character of fantasy in what is otherwise a realistically presented novel. Fantasy, like the other subgenres related to it, may be and often is used to comment on issues and themes of importance to readers in the real worlds they inhabit.

One very important and popular subdivision of fantasy is science fiction, which most properly refers to novels and stories containing some element of science or technology in setting, plot, or situation. Thus science fiction is often set in the future, when scientific or technological advances create startling new possibilities for adventure and allow writers to illuminate old human and social problems in new ways as well as to predict outcomes of present conditions. The term "science fiction," however, is often used rather loosely to refer to all works set in the future whether or not they contain important scientific or technological components. Thus the term may be used to refer to stories taking place at some future time which have little technical interest but instead concentrate on social or political structures and their impact on life. This particular type shades into what is known as the "utopia" and its darker companion, the "dystopia."

First historically and logically of this pair is the utopia. Named for the mythical country created by Sir Thomas More in his book called *Utopia*, which dates from 1516, books in this subgenre depict advanced societies which have solved problems current in their authors' own times. Though these imagined ideal societies may be claimed to exist in hidden places (the middle of the earth, on distant islands) or in a lost past (Atlantis), they are usually set in a future which is presented as having developed beyond problems of the present. By contrast with what readers know to be the situation of their own world, readers of a utopian work are shown both what is wrong with their society and what could be done to fix it. Examples of utopias come primarily from the elite culture and span the years from More's influential work through Sir Francis Bacon's *New Atlantis* (1627) and Samuel Butler's *Erewhon* (1872) to Edward Bellamy's *Looking Backward* (1888) and William Dean Howells' *A Traveler from Altruria* (1894).

Interestingly, the utopian form has not attracted writers of popular novels in large numbers nor has it been particularly influential during the twentieth century. The contrasting form, the dystopia, has instead become important during that time and within popular literature. In doing the opposite from the utopia, the dystopia presents a society, usually set in the future, which carries to extremes tendencies present in the author's society against which the author wishes to warn her or his readers. Among well-known dystopias are Aldous Huxley's *Brave New World* (1932), George Orwell's *1984* (published in 1949, well before its title date), and Margaret Atwood's *The Handmaid's Tale* (1986). The dystopia seems more congenial to our period than the utopia, perhaps an indication of the pessimism about the future of humanity, which has followed on such twentieth-century experiences as Nazism and the Holocaust, World War II, the dropping of atomic bombs on Hiroshima and Nagasaki, increasing pollution, and so on. McCullough is only one of many writers who have looked to the future to understand what may follow from trends of today.

A Creed for the Third Millennium, McCullough's single book set in the future, is typical for our period in being a dystopia, not a utopia. Trends of pollution and population growth as well as of increasing centralization of political power have, in this vision of a future only a few decades away, created a situation in which daily life has become difficult and psychological depression has become epidemic. McCullough, in the manner of most dystopian writers, uses narrative and exposition (that is, storytelling and direct analysis) to depict this future. What she is most interested in is the attempts to find solutions for the psychological problems created by the physical and political situations. Thus her dystopia centers on a proposed "creed" or belief system and a potential charismatic leader. What the novel demonstrates are the danger of corruption of the leader when power and acclaim comes to him and the possibility of misuse of a basically good set of values when they are not rightly understood.

HISTORICAL FICTION

Historical fiction is a genre with a well-defined history of its own. It is usually said to have begun in the late eighteenth century, in the same period when the novel itself developed into its modern forms. The single author whose name and work are always referred to as shaping the form, if not actually creating it, is Sir Walter Scott. Other well-known writers of historical fiction listed by McCullough, along with Scott, are Bulwer Lytton, Lew Wallace, Gore Vidal, Margaret Mitchell, and Jean Auel (McCullough "Reflections" 1).

Just as fantasy and science fiction and their related types obviously contain created worlds which represent realms of the imagination—in space or in the future, perhaps—so historical fiction contains created worlds that represent the past. Thus historical novelists try to recreate what actually has existed rather than to pretend about what might come to be. Such novels are based on research rather than on the imagination. Two main issues for the writer and critic of historical fiction are the time of the action and the degree of closeness to actual events.

The terms "historical fiction" and "historical novel" both refer, of course, to two aspects of this sort of writing: the fact that it is historical and that it is fiction. It might be argued that any fiction set at a time prior to the moment which the writer is describing is historical, but this definition would be so loose as to be useless. In practice, and often without particularly examining our procedure, we limit the use of the term "historical fiction" to stories occurring so far previous to the time of writing that the author must do research in order to depict that world. Of course, it must be admitted that many writers do research in order to depict aspects of society that are not personally familiar to them; the mere studying of one's topic in order to get it right is not sufficient. One possible general rule might be that a work is historical if it is set prior to the author's birth. Thus *An Indecent Obsession,* while set in a particular time earlier than the moment of composition and relying on its position in time to make its setting and action possible, is not truly historical since its occurrence at the end of World War II places it in a time known to its author from her childhood and familiar to many of her first readers from their own knowledge. On the other hand, the early portions of *The Thorn Birds* are clearly historical, since their setting in New Zealand and Australia, at the time of World War I, places them in a time known only by hearsay or by reading to McCullough and her readers.

This may seem a rather trivial point, and one might ask why it matters to a reader whether the author had to do research on a novel's historical period or whether readers have first-hand knowledge of the time in which a work occurs. However, it is significant, since lack of personal familiarity with historical conditions or information presents certain problems and opportunities to author and reader. It automatically ensures that there will be a sort of doubleness of perception of the materials of the work. Author and reader will relate to the work from the perspective of their own time, bringing the value judgments and attitudes, for example, of the late twentieth century to the customs and behaviors of citizens of the Roman Republic and judging harshly the cruel brutality taken for granted within the novels. As McCullough has observed, morality and ethical standards vary markedly from age to age. This view from outside the work is inescapable, no matter how hard both author and reader may try to suspend their own feelings and attitudes. At the same time, though, they will attempt to feel their way into the minds and emotions of the characters of the period being written about, and thus they will also get from the work a perception of what it was like to live at that particular time and under those special conditions. McCullough admits to "loving the people I am writing about." She also reminds us "that Then is not Now," but also "that Then bears a startling relevance for those of us who live Now" ("Reflections" 4). Similar doubleness of feeling and attitude may be connected with fantasy and science fiction and, of course, are important to utopian and dystopian fiction. They become particularly obvious, however, with historical fiction since with this genre the reader and author are connecting with two separate actualities at once, not with one actuality and one imaginary world.

Just as significant as the "historical" aspect of this genre is its "fiction" aspect. The distinction between straight history and historical fiction is clear, but historical fiction varies greatly in the proportions of historical reporting and fictitious narrative it contains. There is a gradual line leading from fiction which is very heavily historical, containing little that is imagined, to fiction which is almost entirely fictional, with the former time of its occurrence being its major historical characteristic. Along this line, novels and stories could be observed with widely differing emphases on their historical content. Some are principally fictions, with little appearance of actual historical personages and relatively unimportant use of historical events. In these works, historical background is used mainly to give flavor to the story, and the main concern is for accuracy about details of daily life. Western novels set along the American frontier in the last years of the nineteenth century often exemplify this approach.

More historical are novels in which historical figures appear and in which historical events form important parts of the plot, while fictitious characters and their imagined adventures serve as the central interest. Nathaniel Hawthorne's *The Scarlet Letter* (published in 1850 but set 200 years earlier) is one example, although its use of historical figures as minor characters is slight. Somewhere in the middle are novels like Margaret Mitchell's *Gone with the Wind* (1936), in which actual battles and other events of the Civil War impinge harshly on the lives of created characters. This is the type most readers probably think of first when the genre of historical fiction is mentioned.

Most historical, and relatively unusual, are novels which are nearly straight history in that actual people are the main characters, and real events form the plot, with imagined characters and people being included only when necessary to flesh out and explain and motivate the history. This is sometimes history made easy for the reader, lacking the examination of sources and arguments about theories which characterize much straight historical writing. The author of the fiction determines what her or his interpretation of that history is, conveys that interpretation using ordinary fictional methods and techniques, and tries to make the past come alive by creating whatever is necessary in addition to the known facts. Authors who are serious about their history and who want to clarify their uses of sources and defend the accuracy of their fictionalizing often append to their novels introductions or afterwords, many times with bibliographies of serious historical sources.

McCullough made several very different uses of historical materials in her fiction. In *The Thorn Birds,* the opening sections occurring in the early years of the World War I are historical principally in making use of a past era as background for their action. Social conditions and details of daily life for members of the working class in New Zealand and physical difficulties of life on a large sheep station in Australia are the main concerns. The characters of the novel have no real connection with the greater world and world events occurring during these years, and little mention is made of them. The historicity of this portion of the novel is found mainly in its evocation of what life was like then and there for people like the Clearys, the family who are McCullough's subject.

Much more historical in several ways are the novels in McCullough's Roman series. Here we have almost straight history with fictionalization occurring in the creation of dialogue, the revelation of characters' thoughts and feelings, and the imagining of episodes and minor characters which help to portray major characters and explain why they act as they must. McCullough is deeply serious about her historical thoroughness and accuracy, and each of the Roman novels is accompanied by additional materials which are intended both to defend them as soberly accurate and to help the reader understand them in their historical context. Information about prior history is included, as are extensive glossaries of Latin terms, historical phenomena, and legal, social, and technical practices unfamiliar to the twentieth-century reader. Occasionally in her prefatory material or glossaries, she indicates that certain interpretations she has chosen are not usually accepted and gives some indication why she has chosen a particular approach. Maps and occasionally diagrams are provided, and portraits of major characters, taken where possible from known statues, are included. A bibliography of sources is not supplied but, she says, may be obtained from her publisher. All this suggests that McCullough's goal in these novels is to provide a wide popular audience with a firm and accurate understanding of a complex and fascinating period in ancient history.

As her career has progressed, McCullough has turned away from using her native Australia for her main settings. She was no longer living in Australia by the time her writing career began, and after her first several successes she has generally used other settings. *Tim* and *The Thorn Birds* are set in Australia, and *An Indecent Obsession* is set nearby among Australian characters. Of later novels, only *The Ladies of Missalonghi,* unusual in other ways, is set in the author's own homeland; *A Creed for the Third Millennium* is set in the United States in the twenty-first century, and the Roman novels take place in the ancient world.

More significant observations about the progress of McCullough's literary career relate to her refusal to restrict herself to any one popular genre and a certain increase in her seriousness of purpose. She began as a writer who wished for the sales which would give her comfort and security. *The Thorn Birds* was partly the result of a rather careful study of what succeeded followed by the conscious creation of a book that would satisfy the market she had analyzed. *Tim,* whose creation overlapped with that of *The Thorn Birds,* helped her begin to establish herself, and then *The Thorn Birds* achieved a blockbuster success that made possible the rest of her career. Both those two early novels, however, rise above their origins in practicality, for each is original in its own way.

With *An Indecent Obsession,* McCullough turned to writing what might be called a "theme" novel or a "novel of ideas." Using romance and mystery elements, she constructed a psychological novel which develops themes of guilt and responsibility. Where themes in *The Thorn Birds* inhere in characters and plotting, they are less important than the interesting story McCullough tells there. In *An Indecent Obsession,* on the other hand, the themes are the reason for the story's existence. Sister (nurse) Langtry and the men she cares for have been created to illustrate the themes.

With the exception of *The Ladies of Missalonghi,* the books after *An*

Indecent Obsession continue to reveal the increasing depth of intellectual concern begun in that third novel. *A Creed for the Third Millennium* takes as its purpose the analysis of a terrible future the world may face, and the Roman novels survey in great detail an important but today little-known period in ancient history. Only *The Ladies of Missalonghi,* a short and frivolous novel, contradicts this trend. However, even that novel, insofar as it parodies some of the elements of the romance form and perhaps one particular romance novel, may be seen as a kind of declaration of her independence from the formulaic fiction her work had been related to but never confined within.

3

Tim
(1974)

McCullough's career as a novelist began with a relatively short novel, which is quite different from the book for which she is best known. *Tim* does not fit easily into one of the categories of genre popular fiction. As a "mainstream" novel, it does not need to follow particular conventions of such genres as the mystery or science fiction, though it does fit loosely into the romance form. It purports to be an examination of a particular social problem in a particular place in the present. The dedication, to a physician serving as chair of the Yale University School of Medicine Department of Neurology, suggests a concern on McCullough's part for accuracy in her depiction of mental retardation. A contemporary retelling, in reverse, of the Pygmalion story, which depicts a strong male creating a weak female in the image he chooses (popularized most recently in the play and film of *My Fair Lady*), this first novel is an example of the maturation story and is original and inventive in several important ways.

Published in 1974, *Tim* is an interesting examination of the relationship of a mentally retarded young man and the middle-aged woman who befriends him. It is based on an unlikely plot: intelligent and highly competent middle-aged woman falls in love with and marries a young man with the mentality of a child. As a love story which depicts a courtship leading to marriage, it follows the basic story line of the romance. It may also be read as a double maturation or education novel, a genre based on the initiation of the protagonist, or central character, to aspects of the human condition or of society which he or she must know in order to cope with the world. In this novel, both the protagonist, Mary Horton, and the title character, Tim, are incomplete, and each must grow and change. They are presented as almost direct opposites, his flaws being mental and hers emotional. The novel shows them becoming complementary in some respects. At the same time, as we will see in the alternative reading to follow, the novel may be read as having antiromance elements, like much of McCullough's work, since the expected roles of male and female are reversed.

As a novel, *Tim* is ultimately unsuccessful because its conclusion resolves little and the basic plot and characterization are unconvincing. It was quickly written, in an attempt to earn needed money, and McCullough has scornfully referred to it as "my bucket of tears book" (Steinberg 110) and as "saccharine-sweet" (Cassill 35). Reviewers differed, most referring to the basic plot as unbelievable but finding some freshness in the treatment. It contains some effective scene drawing, some nice touches of characterization, a stimulating reversal of expectations about social roles as they relate to both gender and mental capacity, an evocative use of the Australian scene, and some interesting plotting.

PLOT DEVELOPMENT

The basic plot of *Tim* concerns a mentally retarded but physically beautiful young man of twenty-five who is first befriended and then married by a sexually repressed woman of forty-three. The novel has a simple basic structure (that is, organization) that falls naturally into two main sections. The first, and longest, approximately the first eighteen chapters, concerns the meeting and growing friendship of Tim Melville and Mary Horton. The second main structural section of the novel, approximately chapters nineteen to twenty-eight, the end of the book, begins when the death of Tim's mother necessitates that some provision be made for Tim's future, changing—or clarifying—the relationship between Tim and Mary. The first section relies heavily on ambiguity, questioning repeatedly whether their relationship is principally that of a surrogate mother and child or is of a romantic and potentially sexual nature. In fact, as the section proceeds, both aspects of the relationship grow in intensity. The second section, centering on Mary's decision to marry Tim as the only way to ensure his future security, redefines their relationship while dramatizing its gradual deepening into a fully rounded marital intimacy. However, the novel's last pages cast doubt on whether that relationship can ever be completely accepted by society. In fact, it can be argued that the novel actually contains two alternative endings: chapter twenty-seven provides an optimistic resolution to the book's issues, and chapter twenty-eight undercuts it by adding an unrelated episode which creates an ending that denies that optimism. In any case, by the end of the novel, both Tim and Mary have grown and matured, though in different ways, and they are able to form a marital relationship which will be mature on the physical and emotional level, though never on the intellectual. Tim's education is sexual and emotional, and Mary's is emotional and social.

The plot moves in a series of alternating steps, almost like a dance in which first Mary and then Tim acts or takes some sort of initiative. Mary's actions tend to forward what might be called the external plot: she opens their relationship by hiring Tim to work for her, she invites him to visit her first at her Artarmon home and then at her beach cottage, and she decides that they will marry. Tim's behavior tends to move what might be called an internal plot, beginning physical contact between them on several occasions. The external plot concerns those aspects of their relationship observable by the outside world, while the internal plot concerns its psychological and purely personal dynamics. Mary acts with full consciousness of what she is doing (though not always in full awareness of all of the implications of her actions), while Tim acts instinctively (usually without awareness of the meaning or potential consequences of what he is doing). Mary acts, but Tim reacts.

From the beginning, there are ambiguities in Mary's response to Tim. She is struck by his beauty and quite intentionally strikes up a connection with him. When she quickly realizes that his beautiful body is inhabited by a child's mind, she perceives the body as vacant. She feels sorry for him, and for some time her behavior is motivated partly by pity. But she is struck by his good-natured response to her overtures. He is flattered by her attention and grateful for her kindnesses. She is attracted to him, and his beauty is central to that attraction, but whether the attraction is maternal or romantic and sexual is long unclear. She employs him as her gardener, and gradually she draws him into her life. She brings him into her house, feeds him, and enjoys his admiration of her home and lifestyle. Soon she asks permission of his parents, Ron and Esme Melville, to take him to her cottage, and there their relationship deepens. She never meets the parents, conversing with them only by telephone, and Tim has persuaded them that she is quite elderly, as he himself naively believes because of her white hair. Before very long, she is reading about mental retardation, and she begins teaching him to read and write. Eventually, she even consults John Martinson, a teacher who specializes in working with the retarded, about what his potential might be. As all this continues, Ron and Esme see her influence on Tim as completely good and are pleased by it. His sister Dawn, on the other hand, becomes jealous of Tim's wholehearted devotion to Mary.

The first major crisis of the novel comes when Dawn announces her engagement. Significantly, that announcement immediately follows the Melvilles' discovery of Tim's newly acquired ability to read and write. In this evening which is so momentous for her, Dawn feels somewhat displaced, for her joyous announcement is overshadowed by Tim's triumph. Dawn's engagement and marriage are most important in forcing Tim to learn about separation and in introducing the idea of the permanent separation, death. He feels that Dawn's approaching marriage is a desertion of him, and he is angry and resentful. As happens consistently from now on, Mary is the one who must try to make him understand such concepts of mature human life. A crucial scene shows her attempting to convey to him the notion that Dawn will still love him and that her marriage will be a happy occasion but that it will also be one of many partings which will precede the final inevitable parting in death. Early in this scene, as Tim was at his most uncomprehendingly distraught, she had hugged him. As the scene ends, they discuss the hug and she defines it as "comforting" him, a term he picks up and uses, not always appropriately, for some time to come. Clearly, that "comforting," that close physical contact, is an early step toward the greater physical contact which will come later. Dawn, despite the misgivings of her socially prominent in-laws-to-be, insists that Tim attend her wedding, but Ron and Esme protect him from the social exposure that the reception would bring. At their request, Mary picks him up after the wedding and takes him to her cottage. She is now so much a part of Tim's life—even though Ron, Esme, and Dawn have never seen her in person—that she becomes involved in such intimate family problems as this.

Dawn's desertion by marriage is followed by another, and more final, loss, Esme's sudden death by a heart attack. Wedding and funeral motifs are contrasted with each other, though both move the plot inexorably toward Tim's shift from his family to Mary. Esme's death and the problems it brings to the fore had been frequently foreshadowed by emphasis on Ron's and Esme's advanced ages (they were already middle-aged when he was born). When it does occur, Tim is shaken, but he has to some degree been prepared for the event by Mary's discussion with him of the meaning of death. Ron thinks it best for Tim not to attend the funeral; again, Mary is asked to take him for that time. The ensuing scene draws together a number of plot threads and instigates the rest of the action. This time, instead of Mary's finding Tim sitting on a wall waiting for her, as had occurred after the wedding, she comes to the Melville house to pick him up. Thus for the first time, finally, she comes face to face with the Melvilles, and their shock at discovering that she is not as elderly as Ron and Esme, as they had fondly believed, is immense. That shock particularly affects Dawn. Long suspicious of Mary's motives, she now becomes absolutely convinced that they are perverted and sexual, that Mary had simply wanted Tim as her lover. She brutally accuses Mary of this. Ron is horrified and apologetic, and Tim is uncomprehending but rather surprisingly takes charge, breaks up an incipient fight between Ron and Dawn's husband, and brings at least a strained peace.

All this is most significant for establishing Dawn's hostility and for suggesting the sorts of suspicion and innuendo that Mary can expect if she continues her interest in Tim. At the same time, it leads into her decision to do just that. Ron is utterly bereft without Esme. Her death reminds him of Tim's vulnerability and the need to secure his future. But her death also destroys his will to live. He realizes that Dawn should not be depended upon to care for her brother. In the meantime, as a result of Dawn's accusations, Mary is becoming more aware of the ambiguity of her feelings for Tim. For the first time, when she bathes him and puts him to bed after he has soiled himself while sick, she sees him naked and is aware of behaving somehow "furtively" (169), perhaps even pruriently, in her reaction to his nudity. Everything that makes it dangerous—especially from Mary's point of view—for them to continue their relationship is becoming increasingly apparent. At the same time, the need for action which will protect and ensure Tim's future is becoming ever more obvious.

Always aware of their age, Ron and Esme had long ago provided for Tim's financial security. But the question of where and how he would live must now be decided. Ron settles it by asking Mary to care for him, and she immediately agrees. That step forward, however, is followed by a step backward. Tim does not know that Ron and Mary have been discussing his future, and he withdraws from Mary into an unexplained resentment. When Mary teases the reason from him, it turns out that he has been jealous of Mary's concern for Ron. His jealousy parallels Dawn's jealousy of Tim's liking for Mary, and the results are equally dramatic. Mary persuades him that she loves him no less simply because she is concerned for Ron and explains that Ron is going to die because he now has nothing to left to live for. Tim is overjoyed to realize that Mary truly does care most deeply for him, and in his elation he imitates the films he has seen on television by seizing and kissing her. While they have kissed each other before—chaste good-night kisses on the forehead—this is their first adult and sensual kiss. Mary responds, partly involuntarily because she is physically aroused and partly out of a sense that she must not reject him at this vulnerable moment. But their relationship is inevitably changed by the kiss, and the physical and sexual component of their relationship cannot henceforth be denied. However, frightened and aware of dangerous implications, Mary persuades Tim that the kiss was a "sin" for people in their situation (with their differences in age and mentality) and that it must not be repeated. Acquiescing, Tim repeatedly states that he now belongs to Mary. He has completely transferred his allegiance from his birth family to her, and it is clear that this new allegiance is based partly on his newly found sexual adulthood, an adulthood which he only dimly understands but which Mary is aware of as a new and disturbing element in their relationship.

Mary's dilemma now is how she can care for Tim and also protect him and herself. Dawn is a potential threat. As a blood relative, she could contest Ron's will and obtain control over the money set aside for Tim. Her deep suspicion of and anger at Mary make that a real danger. Mary could not adopt him, since he is legally an adult. In her quandary, she again visits John Martinson, the teacher of the retarded, and that minor character now plays a crucial role. In fact, his earlier appearance served mainly to prepare for his function at this point in the novel. He hears her out, asks a number of penetrating questions which elicit the entire story from her, and then tells her that the only solution is for her to marry Tim. Startled, she resists his suggestion, but she is finally persuaded by his argument that Tim deserves as full a life as he can experience, that he can experience full sexuality, and that she owes him his "manhood."

From this point, the novel moves quickly to its ending. Mary informs Ron of her decision to marry Tim, explaining in an almost self-sacrificing manner that the most important thing is Tim's life and she will do anything—including marrying him—to make that life as full as possible. She also informs Archie Johnson, her employer, and Mrs. Parker, her neighbor, both of whom, like Ron, support her decision and wish her happiness. Even Tim's boss and her gynecologist are told before Tim! Finally, she tells Tim, in the third of the scenes in which she explains a life-changing event to him. It is ironic that he is the last to be told what his fate is to be, and yet as Mary is leading him toward the conclusion, he anticipates her by asking why they can't get married—since he already belongs to her!

Mary behaves with an extreme objectivity that seems almost a caricature of the emotional control portrayed in the opening pages of the novel. This behavior may be typical of what she was, perhaps, but it is certainly surprising in a sudden bride. She goes immediately from the wedding to the hospital to have her tubes tied (she does not wish to repeat the mistake of Esme and Ron in bearing a child at her advanced age) and to have her sexual organs prepared so that she will not disturb Tim by showing pain when their marriage is consummated. She spends several weeks at the hospital quite unnecessarily so that she will be fully recovered and ready to receive Tim as her lover when she returns home. As a result of her calculated actions and of Ron's preparing Tim by explaining the sex act, their reunion is blissfully beautiful and their experience of sex is passionate and fulfilling. Ron soon dies, probably from intentional starvation, but Mary comforts Tim and finds an almost mystical comfort in having been aware, she thinks, of the moment of Ron's death.

The next-to-last chapter of the novel concludes with a statement which affirms the continuance of life and the primacy of love. At this point, the issues of the novel seem resolved, and the plotlines have come to a natural and optimistic ending, almost a happy-ever-after conclusion. This is the natural ending of the novel as a romance. McCullough appears to be indicating that, despite all the imbalances in their relationship and despite the social disapproval they can expect, Mary's and Tim's marriage will solve their principal problems and will bring them joy. Love conquers much.

But one more short chapter follows, destroying the sense of closure (of finality) brought by the preceding chapter. Ferrari rightly refers to this chapter as an anticlimax following the real ending of the novel (60). It opens with Ron's funeral, which Mary persuades Tim not to attend. As always, he is protected from appearing at social rituals. A confrontation with Dawn occurs just after the burial, reminding Mary and the reader just how intense public scrutiny and how strong suspicion of her very unconventional marriage will be. Then an entirely new and unexpected event undercuts the earlier sense of completion even further. Tim, always physically adept, accidentally cuts himself quite seriously and must be hospitalized. All the hospital staff assume that Mary, whom they know only as "Mrs. Melville," is his mother, not his wife. Angered and hurt, she realizes that their mistake is quite natural, and she must force herself into composure when, in the last lines of the novel, she prepares to take Tim home. This ending, which suggests that the first "ending" is falsely optimistic, restores the tone of ambiguity and uncertainty that had pervaded much of the development of the novel. One reviewer has noted this structural problem, suggesting that "the novel really ends before Colleen McCullough ends it." This reviewer indicates that Tim's cutting himself is anticlimactic and suggests several possible meanings for that episode (that even Tim's beauty is imperfect or that "the world will always misconstrue this strange looking relationship"), and she finds the episode "superfluous" (Ferrari 60). Tim and Mary may have found sexual fulfillment and they may complement each other in many ways, but they are different in other ways that matter intensely to society. And perceptions of these differences may be expected to soil their love in the future as in the past. Love cannot conquer all.

CHARACTER DEVELOPMENT

Two central characters and several minor ones move the plot and themes in *Tim*. Mary Horton, of course, is the protagonist, or central character, and Tim Melville is almost equal in importance. Secondary to these two are the members of Tim's family—his parents Ron and Esme and his sister Dawn. Additional characters, such as Mary's boss and his wife, her neighbor, the teacher she consults about Tim's potential to learn, and a few others, are more briefly depicted.

Tim is a novel that is largely driven by character. McCullough has defended her presentation of characters in the novel, stating that they were drawn from life.

> I've had patients like him [Tim] for years. The British old maid? I worked with so many of them! Every ward in every hospital in the British Emm-pah is headed by an old maid like Mary Horton—don't laugh—who takes off all her clothes to go to the bathroom. The people Tim worked for were like

people in the building trade who were my father's colleagues.
(Cassill 34, 36)

Depicting the maturation of two contrasting characters, the book concentrates primarily on Tim and Mary and on the beginning and deepening of their relationship. The principal weaknesses of the book are related to this fact. The basic premise, that a sensible, middle-aged spinster would fall in love with a mentally retarded young man, is not very believable, and the resulting characterizations of Mary and Tim are not very compelling. Unfortunately, the most believable of the characters are those who do not need to change and develop. Ron and Esme and Mrs. Parker, even Dawn, all come alive as Mary and Tim do not.

Of crucial importance are the contrasts between Mary and Tim and their growth and change. Both characters are imperfect, lacking in essential abilities or skills. Tim's handicap is obvious, his mental deficiency, and Mary's is more subtle but little less obvious. She is emotionally stunted. Her sexuality, indeed all her capacity to connect with other people, is repressed. Tim's defect is congenital (that is, present from birth). His parents were in their forties when he was born, and doctors have explained his IQ of about 75 as a result of the atrophy of Esme's ovaries (which were working just fine, however, when Dawn was born a year after Tim—Esme explains that his birth restored their function). He is, in the Australian slang he uses to describe himself, "not the full quid." Paradoxically, while seemingly cursed by his mental incapacity, Tim is gifted with striking beauty. Comparisons with Greek statuary are frequently invoked to convey the heroic—and deceiving—quality of that beauty. It is both a blessing and a potential curse: his parents observe the powerful effect his appearance has on women and fear his being taken advantage of sexually. Thus they have shielded him, strengthening the natural innocence—in the sense of lack of knowledge as well as of freedom from evil—that characterizes him. And thus they initially are suspicious of Mary's motives in befriending him. Only his assurance that she is old, that she has white hair, reassures them.

The first impression everyone has of Tim is one of his remarkable beauty. He is frequently likened to a Greek statue, and other classical allusions (references to Narcissus, Oberon, and Morpheus, for example) are used to define his appearance. When Mary first sees him, she is "dumbfounded" (9) by that beauty. Her second observation of him only strengthens her wonder. As McCullough describes it, "Mary stood in lost loneliness watching him, not aware of herself, not conscious that she was possessed by an emotion alien to her whole being, neither guilty nor confounded" (22). This brief passage accomplishes two things. It reinforces the emphasis on Tim's beauty by presenting its power on another person, and it begins the process of developing Mary's attraction to Tim despite her inhibited nature.

Tim's innocence is dramatically emphasized in the opening pages of the novel in a scene which McCullough has said "came straight out of real life" (Cassill 36), when his coworkers on a builder's crew play a cruel trick on him. They substitute feces for sausage in a sandwich and laugh at him when he not only does not react to the unexpected taste but does not know what they mean when they explain that he has just eaten a "turd sandwich." The scene functions, as McCullough has said, as "a true and shocking way to show Tim's mentality" (Cassill 36). Appearing to be a mature—and strikingly handsome—man, Tim is mentally and emotionally a child. Good natured, quick but shallow in his emotional reactions, he is a reliable worker for his builder-employer and for Mary Horton when she hires him as her gardener. He loves and is loved by his family. Ron and Esme have done a good job in rearing him to be as independent as possible, given his limitations, and they also shelter and protect him. He is cherished by his sister Dawn, whom he always refers to as "my Dawnie," a bright young woman with good prospects who tries to include him in her life as much as she can. The potential problem, of course, is that Ron and Esme are already elderly and Dawn needs to live her own life. Such concerns do not occur to Tim until they are forced into his consciousness. Dawn's engagement, marriage, and pregnancy move her to the edges of Tim's life, and then Esme's death and Ron's awareness of his own mortality complete the rupturing of his family. And these events help to force Tim to learn about his vulnerability.

Like Tim, Mary Horton is an incomplete person, not fully mature. When the novel opens, she is presented as a stereotypical old maid. Her repressions and inhibitions may be understood in light of her unfortunate past. Where Tim is blessed with a warm and loving working-class family, Mary has had none and has built a comfortable life by determination and hard work. Her experience—reared in an orphanage, independent from the age of fourteen, working as typist and then secretary for a mining company from the age of fifteen—has taught her not to trust others or to become intimate with them. However, she has succeeded dramatically, becoming the private secretary to the managing director of her firm, saving and investing from her modest salary, and achieving financial independence. By the time her story begins, she owns her own home in a prosperous suburb, drives an expensive car, and possesses a beach cottage with surrounding acreage. She continues to work but indulges herself in many luxuries and has never had or been interested in having male companionship. In a cliché of both fiction and popular culture, her repressed sexuality is symbolized by her prematurely white hair, which she wears in a tight bun. In a related cliché, the beginning of her sexual awakening is symbolized by the loosening of her hair after she has been swimming and by Tim's admiring and touching it.

Parallelling the incident with the turd sandwich, which dramatizes Tim's innocence, is a brief episode which suggests Mary's initial rigid and habit-ridden existence. As she leaves for work one morning, she is irritated by the loud and shrill noise of cicadas. As she does each morning, she removes her gloves, uncoils her garden hose, and drenches the bushes from which the insects are humming. Silence ensues—except from one "cicada choirmaster," as he is always called. She reacts with anger but admits defeat, redons her gloves, and goes off to work. She has conquered her origins and won through to prosperity, and she attempts, with only partial success as the battle with the cicadas shows, to control her environment. Control of herself and her world is typical of Mary as she is initially characterized.

Development of the two characters shows each changing and growing in ways that make them more rounded and whole. Mary learns the emotion, even passion, that she had lacked. Tim cannot, of course, increase his intelligence, but Mary does help him to take fuller advantage of what he has by teaching him basic literacy skills. Both characters learn to express the adult sexuality that had been latent in each of them. At the end of the book, both are able to live together a fulfilling life that would not have been possible before they met and changed each other. For each, then, the novel depicts a maturation experience.

Several other characters play significant supporting roles in the development of the novel. Most important, and the most effectively and believably depicted characters in the book, are Tim's parents and sister. Ron and Esme have been good parents to Tim, protecting him when they could, helping him learn independence when it was possible, and preparing for his future financial security. They are members of the working class and live in a different world from Mary's, but they observe her good influence on Tim and are delighted.

Their relationship with each other is deep and loving but also humorous. Each has his or her own pursuits. Esme has her friends and her tennis, while Ron has his "mates" (in the Australian slang) at the neighborhood bar. The depth of their mutual dependency becomes clear after Esme's death when Ron has no more desire to live. He sees to it that Tim will be safe, thus fulfilling Esme's final request, and then he dies. They are earthy, honest, and affectionate, but limited by their lack of education and experience.

Dawn's characterization is more complex than that of Ron and Esme. Early in the novel, she is quite favorably depicted. Tim's affection for her establishes her worth, as does her love for him and her insistence that he be included in important family occasions. Tim's name for her, "my Dawnie," reveals the affection she has earned from him. She is bright and has a good job. Like Tim she is physically attractive, but the contrast between Tim's retardation and her intelligence is stark. She seems, in fact, to have everything, and her announcement that she will marry her boss, Mick Harrington-Smythe, comes as no surprise to anyone except the members of her family. Tim is startled because he never expects anything in his world to change, and Ron and Esme are shocked because they have never met Mick and because they are strongly aware of the class differences between Dawn and the Harrington-Smythes, whose hyphenated name indicates their class-conscious snobbishness. Ron and Esme try to caution her, feeling that these differences are simply too great. But Dawn has no qualms about her ability to get along with both her husband-to-be and his aristocratic parents. What is more, she intends to do this without betraying her family and origins. In a scene which dramatizes some of her most admirable qualities, she insists to the Harrington-Smythes that Tim be at her wedding. He is her brother and she is not ashamed of him and will not try to hide him away.

Her weakness is that, like the early Mary, she wants control. And she is accustomed to being the center of Tim's life. He has always said that he "liked" Dawn best of all, and when Mary begins to replace Dawn in his affections, she becomes jealous. She does not so much change during the course of the book, like Tim and Mary, as she is revealed. Early in the novel, she seems a fully sympathetic and admirable character, as her affection for Tim and her refusal to be ashamed of his handicap are emphasized. Ironically, it is perhaps her very brightness and talent, which have made her life so much easier than Tim's, that cause her flaws. Used to having things come easily to her and to being the pampered delight of her family and the focus of Tim's affection, she reacts with anger and resentment when her position as Tim's favorite is threatened. In a great irony, her suspicions of Mary's motives in befriending Tim are incorrect when she first voices them, but later they become correct— though her moral judgment of Mary remains wrong. Marriage into a snobbish aristocratic family reinforces Dawn's less attractive characteristics, and so the pleasant, vital, and loving young woman of the novel's beginning becomes its potential villain. That the change in Dawn's characterization is completely believable attests to McCullough's skill as a storyteller.

Supporting Mary, particularly as she grows closer to Tim, are several minor characters. Her neighbor, Mrs. Parker, is in part a comic character. Though she lives in a prosperous suburb, she has never accepted indoor plumbing, and she is something of a gossip. A good-hearted woman, however, she is kind to Tim from the beginning and defends him against the cruel tricks played on him by the other members of the builder's crew on which he works. She is always sympathetic to both Mary and Tim and, despite her initial surprise, she enthusiastically approves Mary's decision to marry Tim. Similarly, Archie Johnson, her employer, loves to tease her and call her insulting names, but he is fond of her and supports her decisions. He enjoys watching her blossom under the influence of her growing involvement in Tim's life. When he learns that she intends to continue working for him after marrying Tim, he is delighted to come to the wedding. These two characters may be seen as representing a sympathetic public opinion, balanced against the enmity and lack of understanding which Mary fears and Dawn represents.

Finally, John Martinson, the specialist in retardation whom Mary consults twice, is presented as a highly competent, perceptive, and sympathetic professional. However, he exists mainly for his function in moving the plot forward. His first scene, in which he gives Mary some suggestions about teaching Tim, seems to function principally to prepare for his later appearance. And his role in that second scene is to present the idea of marriage between Mary and Tim. No one else could present that idea with his authority or credibility. As the notion comes from a disinterested specialist, Mary can argue with it, thus proving that her motives are pure, and be persuaded. Since the marriage of two such dissimilar characters as Mary and Tim is highly unlikely, McCullough needed a way to persuade the reader—as well as Mary—that it was both acceptable and appropriate. Martinson would seem to have been invented to help McCullough get over this very real problem with her plot.

IMAGERY

A powerful tool of characterization in many novels is imagery, that is the use of comparisons to things that appeal to the senses. Throughout this novel, Tim is repeatedly defined by images associating him with dogs. Mary's neighbor, speaking of Tim, connects "dimwits and dogs" (18). When Mary finds Tim patiently waiting for her after Dawn's wedding, she is struck by the childish loyalty that would keep him obediently there, "like a dog," because someone he loved had so commanded him (118). And when John Martinson is attempting to persuade Mary to marry Tim, he describes him as a "poor, silly creature as simple and faithful as a dog!" (215). These dog images occur at significant points in the narrative—when Tim is initially being characterized; at the moment of his first great loss in Dawn's wedding; and as his fate is being determined. The consistency of this imagery and its obvious connotations are striking. Tim is seen as simple in intelligence, loyal and loving, and obedient. All these are fine qualities, but they are not the qualities of the usual sympathetic human character in a novel.

The incident in which Mary Horton attempts unsuccessfully to silence the cicada introduces insect imagery, which is consistently associated with her and which parallels the dog imagery associated with Tim. In fact, Mary's insect imagery is more pervasive and important as well as more complex. As Tim is first working for Mary, she reveals to him her hatred of the noise made by the cicadas and especially of the "cicada choirmaster." Tim, the innocent, immediately proves that he is in touch with nature in a way that Mary is not, for he immediately and easily catches the cicada. He then asks Mary if she wants him to kill the insect, implicitly pleading with her to spare it. Mary pities both the cicada and Tim, seeing his rapport with it and its beauty, and she tells him to free it. Occurring early in their relationship, this little incident shows Tim influencing Mary's behavior, his persuading her to yield a bit in her desire for control. There is never any doubt that Mary has much to teach Tim, but this incident reveals Tim teaching Mary—and softening her. The complexity of the insect imagery lies partly in its being expanded here to connect also with Tim in a very different way from that in which it connects with Mary. While Mary hates and opposes the insect, Tim is akin to it. While Mary is alienated from the natural world, Tim is a part of it.

But insect imagery is associated with Mary in other ways. In one highly charged incident at Mary's cottage, Tim persuades Mary to over-come her fear of the water and to swim with him (again Tim is teaching Mary). Then an early episode of physical contact occurs when her hair, that symbol of her sexuality, is loosened, and he admires and touches it. She realizes he is beginning to imitate her speech patterns, and she ten-derly observes him sleeping. She had instinctively recoiled when he touched her hair, and he had responded "like a dog which does not know why its master kicked it" (68). Troubled by her observations of Tim's behavior, and more especially by her own responses to him, Mary flees to her private place on the beach. As she goes, she hears an owl's cry and then is frightened by being struck in the face by a spider's web (71). She fears that the spider may be on her, much as she also seems to fear Tim's intrusion into the safety of her ordered life. Her alienation from nature is again stressed and parallels her fears of natural emotion and sexuality. The mention of the spider's web is brief and unemphatic, but it falls into the general pattern of imagery associated with Mary and, interestingly, in this episode it follows quickly after an occurrence of the dog imagery which is typically associated with Tim.

The final important example of insect imagery in association with Mary occurs at the end of the first major section of the novel, just before Esme's death. Again there is a scene in which Tim reaches out to Mary, showing both how much he is coming to depend on her and how vul-nerable he is. Again Mary goes to her beach alone to think. This time the insect is only in her thoughts as she attempts to understand what is happening in her relationship with Tim. The depth of her own feelings and the hopelessness of their situation are emphasized here. She likens herself to a moth and Tim to the light about which the moth flies. He fills her awareness, blocking out everything else, just as the light hyp-notizes and blinds the moth. Like the inanimate light, he has no notion of her feelings or her pain. In melodramatic language, the narrative sum-marizes her thoughts: "she buffeted herself against the walls of his iso-lation" and yearns "to immolate herself on the flame of his fascination" (141). The implications of approaching disaster are inescapable. She is losing control of her own emotions and of the course of their relation-ship. Underlining this point, Tim takes an initiative new to him. He finds her on the beach, comforts her, carries her to her bed, and promises to take care of her. Their roles are, for this moment, reversed. She is the vulnerable, weak one, and he behaves with sensitive and masterful as-surance. Significantly, Tim is nowhere likened to a dog in this passage. Unexpectedly, however, he compares Mary to a "soft and warm" kitten

(142). This breaking of the pattern previously established further emphasizes the changes occurring in these two characters and in their relationship with each other.

SETTING

Setting most obviously refers to the place in which a fiction takes place. In *Tim,* that location is in and near Sydney, Australia. There are descriptions of Australian scenes, including landscape, climate, and plants growing there. The human scene is more important than the geography, however, and both Mary Horton's middle-class suburb of Artarmon and the Melvilles's working-class neighborhood are evoked in some detail. For Artarmon, what is shown is principally Mary's comfortable house and extensive garden and her next-door neighbor's more old-fashioned property. The Melvilles's world is revealed principally through scenes in their home and in the neighborhood tavern which Ron and Tim frequent. Australian dialect, particularly in the language of the Melvilles and Tim's working crew, helps to create a sense of place.

Contrasting with the scenes in Sydney are those at Mary's beach cottage. From the time he first sees it until after the consummation of their marriage, Tim is not comfortable inside Mary's Sydney home, though he admires it and even suggests that she introduce some touches of red into its unrelieved neutral tones. He is always happier outside in her grounds, reinforcing the notion of his communion with nature revealed in the cicada incident. It is significant that their marriage is consummated in the garden, not inside the house.

At the beach cottage, her private retreat never before shared with anyone else, however, he is immediately at home. He delights in swimming and persuades her to join him. This is one of the first examples of his overtly teaching her, of her beginning to cast aside her inhibitions. Her prudishness had been emphasized by the fact that even when alone she had worn girdle and stockings and proper clothing. She does not even have a swimsuit and is forced that first time to swim in her underclothes and a hacked off dress. While swimming, she discovers a feeling of freedom new to her, and afterward she liberates her hair from its usual bun and then sleeps. The symbolism of her beginning sexual liberation is obvious and is made even clearer by Tim's caressing of that loosened hair while she drowses and her terror when she wakes to that caress.

She may be awakening to her sexuality, but she is not yet ready, nor is Tim, to recognize it.

The importance of the cottage as a symbolic setting is underscored by two particularly important scenes in which Mary considers her relationship with Tim. Both come at moments when things are changing for them and when Mary must either come to a decision or learn to understand herself and her feelings. In each scene, she goes alone to the beach at night, sits by a fire, and in solitude considers her situation. The beach for her represents a place of retreat, and it becomes associated with the furthering of her maturation and of her relationship with Tim. The first of these beach scenes immediately follows her swimming and Tim's caressing her loosened hair. Filled with a range of emotions, she thinks back over her past and tries to understand what is happening to her. But she is as confused after her moments of meditation as she had been when she fled there, and the description of her final act on the beach reinforces the ambiguity of her situation. Practicing fire safety, she extinguishes the fire. Unaware of the small creatures harmed by the fire, she puts it out by throwing sand on it, not by dousing it with water. This is, the narrative points out, "safe enough as a fire hazard precaution, but no cooler for the sand and its inhabitants" (75). As always, Mary is separated from the nature of which Tim is so naturally a part.

The second beach scene is more conclusive. After both Dawn's marriage and Mary's first consultation with John Martinson, Tim and Mary are at the cottage, and Mary is troubled by her increasing sense of closeness to Tim and her inability to understand just what he thinks and feels. Needing to be alone, she goes again to the beach, where she gives way to grief and, in a recurrence of the insect imagery associated with her, puzzles through the likeness of herself to a moth flying around Tim as a flame. This time Tim intrudes on her private place and carries her up to bed. The beach's associations enlarge to include Tim at this point, and Mary's isolation is being broken by his innate if unconscious sensitivity.

Two other scenes on the beach, one before and one after the one just described, underscore the unifying associations of that setting. It is on the beach that Mary explains the nature and meaning of separation and death to Tim, and it is there that she explains to him that they will marry. From its initial associations with Mary's loneliness, it is transformed into a place of union for the two of them. The cottage and its surroundings is always a place of refuge—first for Mary and then for Mary and Tim. The beach is the place where those associations are strongest.

Tim as a novel relies heavily on settings. The Australian background, both social and geographical, is well depicted. Additionally, setting is used functionally for the development of plot, character, and themes, principally in the contrast between Mary's home in the suburbs with its associations with society and class and her cottage with its natural surroundings and function as a place of escape.

THEMATIC ISSUES

Themes or abstract ideas in fiction are most effectively presented when they grow naturally from plot and characters. As a romance illustrating maturation, *Tim* has as its central theme the notion of emotional and social growth. The changes in the two central characters obviously dramatize that theme. Usually the maturation novel is constructed around one central character who learns about himself or herself and the world. *Tim* is unusual in that it depicts two characters who must learn contrasting lessons in order to meet at some middle ground. Many maturation novels show failed maturations, in which characters are not enriched by their experiences or in which they are prevented from learning anything which would actually enable them to live fulfilling lives. In this regard, *Tim* is ambiguous. Mary and Tim both grow, and their marriage is presented as happy and passionate. The presence of differing possible endings in the last two chapters is important here. The first possible ending concludes optimistically, emphasizing the joy Tim and Mary take in each other. The second, however, undercuts the optimism of its predecessor by reminding the reader of the power of the outside world to soil their love by misunderstanding it. Maturation has occurred, but whether it is enough is left unclear.

Other themes are related to that primary question of maturation. Some that might be listed are the nature of love and the problems caused by inequalities in love. Those inequalities themselves, such as mentality, age, class, and wealth, also become secondary themes, and each is developed in some detail. The existence of varied kinds of love creates another theme. The novel illustrates romantic love in Dawn and her Mick and in a different way, of course, in Mary and Tim. Familial love is illustrated in the love and concern for Tim of his parents and Dawn. Most importantly, a conflict between kinds of love is shown in Mary's development. For some time, her concern for Tim seems to be a kind of displaced maternal yearning which struggles with a growing sexual attraction to him. Indeed, the resolution—or lack of it—of that struggle is the same as the resolution of the novel. In giving Tim to Mary, Ron has placed his son in Mary's maternal care, and the very nature of Tim's mentality ensures that she will always have to treat him like the child he is. But John Martinson's solution of the problem through marriage and Mary's enthusiastic adoption of it redefines their love as sexual. The second ending of the novel suggests that, even after Mary and Tim are married and the sexual notion of love has come to prevail, society will continue to assume a parent-child relation between them—or to see their sexual resolution as perverted. The study of the nature of love in this book then is ultimately unresolved.

The other primary theme of *Tim* is the very obvious one of mental retardation and the response of society to those who are retarded. This theme is illustrated, of course, in Mary's ambivalences about Tim and her relationship to him. It is also illustrated in the dynamics of the Melville family and in the often thoughtlessly cruel treatment of Tim by his fellow workers. The presence of John Martinson, the teacher of the retarded, gives McCullough the opportunity to convey some specific information about the potential of many retarded persons and about appropriate training and treatment of them. She particularly uses for this purpose Martinson's first appearance, which is otherwise important principally for preparing for his function as introducer of the idea of marriage.

AN ANTIGENERIC READING OF *TIM*

An antigeneric novel functions by establishing some aspects of the genre it is based on, so that readers associate it with that genre and their expectations for other aspects of that genre are established. Then it so alters those other aspects that readers' expectations are violated. The result is an unsettling of responses to the novel, an unsettling that may in fact be the intention of the writer and may be intended to criticize the genre itself, by showing its inherent contradictions or lack of realism.

Tim is based on a courtship plot, like a typical romance novel, and contains a number of other elements of that popular form. But *Tim* reverses or at least alters many of the conventional motifs of the romance. Contemporary romance is aimed at female readers, often though not exclusively at young female readers. Linda K. Christian-Smith has pointed out that reading contemporary popular romances helps to reinforce in their readers many conservative values and attitudes about the roles of men and women in society. While Christian-Smith is discussing romances specifically directed at teenagers and marketed to a mass public, many of her observations about the conservative impact of the romance hold true as well for the form in general. It assumes traditional gender roles, such as an older, more experienced, more powerful male and a younger, inexperienced, often powerless female. If not actually narrated by the heroine, as in the early and very influential *Jane Eyre*, such a novel will be told from the point of view of the heroine, and readers will be expected to identify with her. A courtship leading to the happy ending of engagement or marriage forms the basis of the plot, which often is complicated by doubts or suspicions of the hero's character and motivations. His assertiveness may be both attractive and frightening. The heroine softens him even as he overwhelms her by his passion. The image of Rhett Butler carrying Scarlett O'Hara up the staircase is a familiar example of the relationship many of these novels suggest for their central male and female characters.

Tim contains some elements typical of the romance, most obviously the courtship plot and the use of the heroine's point of view. But these elements are handled very differently from the way typical romance writers would present them. Even—or maybe especially—the ways in which this novel most closely resembles the romance actually work to undercut the assumptions of that genre. For example, most of the novel is seen though Mary Horton's perspective, as the usual romance novel is seen from the perspective—or is told by—the heroine. The use of the female character's point of view seems logically to be controlled less by the patterns of the romance than by the fact that she is the more intelligent of the two characters. If the story were to be told from Tim's perspective, the narrative would necessarily be severely limited by his inarticulateness and inability to comprehend much of what goes on around him. Nevertheless, the centrality of a woman's point of view—even that of a very repressed and inhibited woman—is in keeping with the romance form.

Like point of view, the characterizations of Mary and Tim bear some resemblance to romance heroines and heroes, but the differences are greater and more significant than the similarities. Like a typical romance heroine, Mary is inexperienced sexually and is alone in the world. Like a typical romance hero, Tim is strong and handsome, and eventually he is a tender and passionate lover. Her liberation into a free expression of her emotion is typical of the romance, but his learning his sexual potential is more characteristic of the female than the male role in that genre.

The dog images discussed earlier, which suggest his simplicity, ability to love, and obedience, make him particularly ill-suited for any character—but especially a male character—in a romance. The qualities listed are more usually considered appropriate for the passive romance heroine than for the hero, but the canine imagery is sharply different from the kinds of images most typical of the genre.

In fact, what is most striking about these characters' gender roles is their reversal from the roles of the romance. Mary's assertiveness and strength resemble those of the romance hero, while Tim's dependency and vulnerability are like those of the heroine. Like the conventional hero, Mary is older, more intelligent, assertive, and interested in Tim at first primarily because of his physical appearance. She almost always takes the lead in beginning and developing their relationship. Like the usual heroine, Tim is youthful, strikingly beautiful, innocent of the ways of the world, and generally unassertive. Many of his personality traits are explained by his being mentally retarded, which might be read as an exaggeration of the innocence, even ignorance, of the romance heroine. Perhaps most telling is the way in which his fate is decided. Mary determines that they will marry, makes all the arrangements, and tells her friends. Only then does she inform Tim, utterly certain of what his response will be. His passivity, as extreme as it is, seems an exaggeration of the romance heroine's inability to act. In reversing the gender roles of the principal characters in the conventional romance, *Tim* calls into question the assumptions of that genre.

Tim is in some respects a strikingly original novel. Its central plot device, the love of a stereotyped old maid for a young, mentally retarded man, is startling. McCullough's use of conventions of the romance, often turning them upside down, has the effect of calling into question the assumptions about appropriate qualities and behaviors of characters in those romances and thus the qualities and behaviors taught by the genre. At the same time, the novel conveys information about both mental retardation and the social attitudes regarding it. As a maturation novel, it depicts an unexpected and thus interesting if not always very believable plot of two incomplete persons managing to create between them a relationship that is complete if still unequal.

4

The Thorn Birds
(1977)

McCullough's second published, though her first planned, novel is her greatest success. Published in 1977, it propelled her into the ranks of writers with names recognizable and sought out by readers. The success of her later novels probably depended heavily on the public won by this blockbuster book and the immensely popular television miniseries made from it. Many writers with such popular successes continue to write similar works and thus fall into a personal and recognizable formula, so that a Stephen King novel or a Danielle Steele book promises certain characteristics to a devoted and regular following. McCullough, however, refuses to be placed into any neat pigeonhole, and each new book (or group of books) creates its own type and rules. All this seems, perhaps, a bit paradoxical for an author who had carefully done research into what made a novel succeed with a public of ordinary readers and followed up on her results by creating *The Thorn Birds*. In fact, Breslin calls it "fiction by the numbers" (469). Nevertheless, McCullough's professionalism and her desire for financial success as a writer were clearly instrumental in her first great achievement. That success enabled her to direct the later course of her career as she wished. She will not be restricted to any particular set of readers' expectations. And even in *The Thorn Birds*, she breaks new ground by using a Roman Catholic priest as her dynamic romantic hero.

The usual critical observations about *The Thorn Birds* are that it fits in the category of the family saga and that it is an Australian *Gone with the Wind*. As a family saga, it belongs to a genre which follows several generations of a particular family and thus has several protagonists and covers a lengthy span of years. Describing both the genre and this novel, Clemons calls it "an old-fashioned family saga, featuring decades of tribulation studded with dire forebodings that more often than not come true" (96). Reviewers noticed a number of similarities between McCullough's and Margaret Mitchell's books. Both concern the families, especially the daughters, of Irish immigrant fathers who have come to wealth in their new countries. Both depict large rural estates with beautiful and gracious mansions. Both contain strong-willed heroines who love men they cannot have and marry men who are to them poor substitutes. Both heroines create their own disasters through their shortsighted behavior. And both novels seem made to order for lavish dramatization: *Gone with the Wind* in the 1939 film and *The Thorn Birds* in the 1983 television miniseries. Both, it might be added, reached tremendous audiences as novels, and each made the reputation of its author as a storyteller and creator of strong and fascinating women.

SETTINGS

McCullough's reputation as an Australian author rests principally on *The Thorn Birds*, though she also used Australian settings in *Tim* and *The Ladies of Missalonghi*. The settings of *The Thorn Birds* range widely, although Australia (both New South Wales and Queensland) is the primary locale. Other places used are New Zealand, Rome, London, and Crete. The opening locale is New Zealand, presented as a place of hard labor for working-class families like her subject family, the Clearys. Poverty is their lot. For Paddy, the father and prime supporter of his family, there is the hard and uncertain labor of sheep shearing. For Fiona (Fee), wife and mother of a large and growing family, there is daily drudgery. For their many children, there is schooling under the tutelage of harsh, even sadistic nuns. For none of them does there seem hope of anything better, and there is always the danger of even greater poverty if Paddy cannot get work. These difficult circumstances contrast with the natural beauty of the South Island of New Zealand, described as a green, kindly, and gentle land. There is no apparent future for the Clearys in this lovely place, which in some respects is similar to Paddy's native Ireland, and so the opportunity to emigrate to Australia, especially with the promise of inheriting great wealth from his sister, promises a brighter future than they could have hoped for in New Zealand.

Their arrival in Australia is disheartening. The journey is arduous, and the new country they find is dramatically different from New Zealand in dismaying ways. Where the grass of New Zealand had been lush and green, New South Wales is brown and gray, full of vast, unfenced distances. Dust and dirt will become Fee's constant enemies, and throughout the course of the novel, a cycle of severe droughts and needed but inadequate rains will punctuate their lives. The cruelty of the land is repeatedly stressed, and it ultimately takes Paddy's life in a fire started when lightning strikes trees and brush which are parched and dry from a prolonged drought. Drogheda, however, the sheep station to which the Clearys come, is a refuge and a spot with beauty created by immigrants from a kinder land. The gardens, especially the roses, of the home place on Drogheda are particularly lovely and are but a part of the recreation of European society by the Irish Catholics who have settled this region around the village of Gillanbone. Drogheda comes to be almost a character, and the desire to establish a dynasty of Clearys on this station becomes a driving passion.

If New South Wales contrasted with New Zealand for Fee, then Queensland contrasts with New South Wales for her daughter Meggie. Taken to Queensland as a bride by her new husband, Meggie experiences a lengthy train trip that repeats some of the horror of the family's earlier migration from New Zealand to Australia. Used to the gray and brown of the New South Wales landscape, Meggie at first finds the bright, even garish colors of Queensland almost frightening. Contrasting with the struggle for life of the vegetation in New South Wales, around Dungloe there is a jungle growth with vines and trees and coconut palms everywhere, creating torrents of bright colors. The explanation for this lush growth, of course, is moist tropical heat, which Meggie finds oppressive, a feeling that echoes the oppressive nature of her life in Queensland.

Close by Queensland is Matlock Island, a honeymoon resort, to which Meggie is sent for a vacation when her marriage is broken and she must think through her situation and consider what to do with her life. Matlock is lovely, and her time there becomes idyllic. First she spends time alone, meditating on her life and coming to a decision about her failed marriage. Then there is a romantic and sexual idyll, to be discussed later, which is central to the novel's plot. The setting of the tropical island and the fact that it is associated with young lovers as a honeymoon retreat make it absolutely appropriate for the occurrence of the one purely happy period in Meggie's life.

Other settings are less extensively and importantly used. Rome, or more properly, the Vatican City, is the setting for a number of scenes involving Father Ralph de Bricassart and his rise in the hierarchy of the Roman Catholic Church. Descriptions emphasize the wealth of the Church and the beauty of the surroundings in which its prominent and powerful officers live and do their work. London serves as the setting for the professional striving of Justine, Meggie's actress daughter, but the city is not very fully described. Finally, Crete, the location of the final dramatic event of the novel, the heroic and untimely death of Dane, Meggie's son, is briefly described but is important primarily for the function it plays in the plot—that of allowing Dane to die in a suitably heroic fashion and causing Justine to feel guilt for his death.

Though the settings of the novel range widely, Drogheda and the other Australian places are surely the ones the reader remembers most clearly. Herself an Australian from New South Wales, McCullough was writing about scenes she knew, and her evocation of those landscapes justifies her association with it, even though she has not in fact restricted herself to it in this novel or her other works. Reviewers have almost universally noted the importance of the settings, with most finding them effectively drawn. Two later critics have examined the effectiveness and accuracy of McCullough's Australia in more detail. Morris calls it so full of howlers as to suggest that the novel is a gigantic hoax on the American reading public, but Parasuram has found it faithful and accurate.

PLOT DEVELOPMENT

Centered around three generations of Cleary women, but particularly around the life and passions of Meggie Cleary, *The Thorn Birds* opens by establishing that this is a world in which women suffer and men thoughtlessly cause their pain. The hurts felt by children are particularly pathetic, and McCullough uses this fact to create empathy for Meggie and to set her up as a character who is the helpless victim of men who should protect her. The young Meggie is given a doll, to her a magical creature—the first real gift in her deprived life—and her older brothers, curious about how it works and absolutely insensitive to her feelings, take it from her and nearly destroy it during their investigation of its parts. Meggie's happy moment is ruined and, though her oldest brother Frank, an exception to the heedless cruelty of the Cleary males, rescues it and it is repaired, it is spoiled for her.

Following episodes reinforce this depiction of Meggie as a female who is born to suffer. Her introduction to school is disastrous. Because of her nervousness, she makes herself and her older brothers late. She tries to take responsibility for their lateness, but the nuns, who are portraits of malicious cruelty, punish them all by painfully whipping their hands. As a result, Meggie suffers both physical pain and guilt for having caused her brothers also to be punished. When, out of her wretchedness, she vomits on one of the nuns, her humiliation is complete. This brutal treatment of an innocent child, as well as Meggie's anguished acceptance of her responsibility for the sufferings of others, sets a pattern to be followed throughout the novel.

The principal action of the novel is rather simple, though the novel is long and complex, with many subplots. Basically, the story tells of Paddy Cleary, a poor New Zealand sheep shearer and his large family, who are brought to New South Wales, Australia, by his sister, a wealthy widow with a large sheep station (corresponding to a Western American ranch). She has no children and will make him her heir in return for his managing Drogheda, the station. Paddy's wife, Fee, is from a higher class than he, but she uncomplainingly and competently if dourly manages his household and their children. A local priest, Ralph de Bricassart, becomes enthralled by their young daughter, Meggie. Maliciously, the widow leaves her property to the Church; Ralph is named custodian, and Paddy and his family are given life-time interests and incomes. Ralph and Meggie are in love, but he refuses to break his vow of chastity. He leaves and begins his dramatic rise within the hierarchy of the church. Meggie marries Luke, partly because he reminds her of Ralph. Luke, who loves her money much more than he does her, takes her to western Queensland and a harsh life in which he hires her out as a maid and rarely sees her. She bears Luke a daughter, Justine. Later, her understanding employer sends her off for an island vacation, and Ralph follows her there, where they become lovers and she conceives their son, Dane. She sleeps with Luke one last time, to conceal her baby's actual paternity, and then leaves Luke permanently, returning to Drogheda. There she rears her children, until finally Dane goes to Rome, to become a priest under Ralph's patronage, and Justine goes to London to become an actress. Dane, following in the footsteps of the man he is not aware is his father, is beloved by all and seems destined to become a perfect priest, but while on a holiday in Greece following his ordination, he dies heroically saving another's life. Justine, who feels guilty for not having been with Dane as she had promised, refuses her devoted lover, Rainer, a German businessman and protégé of Ralph's, until finally Meggie persuades her that her true future is with Rainer.

The story is constructed on two bases. First is a situation: a love which is thwarted because the man's priestly vocation makes marriage impossible. Second is a plot device: the will by which Mary Carson leaves her estate to the Church, with Ralph as custodian, thus cheating Paddy and his family—including Meggie—of the inheritance they had been promised. Crucial here is the way in which Mary sets it up. Ralph is forced to decide whether he will do the noble thing and destroy Mary's new will before anyone else knows of its existence or choose to take possession of the estate and thus ensure his future in the Church at Meggie's expense.

The story is narrated in a straightforward chronology, and has, in fact, often been described as an old-fashioned novel, partly for this very reason. It uses the third-person omniscient narrative method typical of the family saga. That is, it is told by an objective outside voice which refers to all characters by third person pronouns, as "she" or "he," and which describes the thoughts and feelings of various characters. McCullough has entitled each of the seven sections of the novel by the dates it covers and by the name of one of the characters. The reason for the attachment of the name of a particular character to a specific section is not always clear, and the order of names in some respects upsets the order of their actual importance in the sweep of the action. But there is an internal logic to these section headings. The order is as follows: Meggie, Ralph, Paddy, Luke, Fee, Dane, and Justine.

Thus the novel opens with Meggie, and her section follows her as a child and young woman. The mature Meggie and her love affair with Ralph are depicted much later, ironically in the section given Luke's name. The fact that Paddy is given a section might be considered surprising, for he is never a principal character and his section comes after he has finished playing a truly important role in the action. His dramatic, terrible, and unnecessary death, however, forms a climax within his section. Luke's name is appropriately on the section which is rounded by Meggie's marriage to him, but the single most important episode in this section is her liaison with Ralph and the conception of Dane. Fee's name is given to a section which comes long after she plays an important role in the action. The titling of this section is perhaps justified by the fact that it is here that she and her daughter Meggie finally come to an understanding and can begin to reveal their affection for each other. Fee's obsessive and fated love for her eldest son comes to its conclusion here, when a defeated and ruined Frank returns to her after serving a long prison term for murder.

The last two sections, titled for Meggie's son and daughter, the third generation of Clearys, are appropriately labeled. Dane's section portrays him as a young adult, shows his fulfillment at his ordination, and depicts his heroic death. The end of the Cleary dynasty on Drogheda is doubly confirmed, first by the vow of chastity taken by the last male of the line and by his death and then in Justine's section, which returns to the female line and shows a Cleary woman who frees herself from the pride of her foremothers and escapes making their mistakes. Thus, though Drogheda is finished as a Cleary empire and the family name will die out, at least there is some fruition to all the suffering of the preceding generations. The novel's last lines return to that idea, stressing the human nature that impels people to grave error.

CHARACTER DEVELOPMENT

The Thorn Birds follows the lives of three women—three generations—of the Cleary family. Fee (Fiona) and her daughter Meggie (Meghann) illustrate the impact in two generations of obsessive love and guilt; Justine (Meggie's daughter), in the third generation finally breaks free of the cycle of suffering. One other female character, Mary Carson, who plays a crucial role in the structure of the book, represents another way in which love—or lust—can destroy. Several male characters (most prominently Paddy, Fee's husband; Father Ralph de Bricassart, Meggie's lover; Luke O'Neill, her husband; and Dane, her son) play important supporting roles and are as fully developed characters as the women. All suffer to one degree or another, and it is in the nature and depth of their suffering that interest partly lies. Of the three women, Meggie is truly central. Fee's story leads up to hers, and Justine's experiences bring closure, finality, to Meggie's. Meggie and Fee alone are present throughout the entire fifty-four-year sweep of the novel, but Fee has faded to a minor character well before the book's end.

Mary Carson's role, played out early in the action of the novel, sets up and contrasts with the experiences of the other three women. When introduced, she is already elderly, a widow for many years and the heir of an immensely rich husband. Drogheda, the sheep station which is the central setting of the novel, represents only a small part of the wealth she controls. Childless and alone in her old age, she sends for her brother, Paddy, to become her head stockman and heir. The two of them, Mary and Paddy, had both left Ireland many years ago to seek their fortunes. Mary, in Australia, had been successful beyond their greatest imaginings, but Paddy, in New Zealand, had never climbed out of the laboring class. Mary is portrayed as a vain, bitter, and angry woman who uses her great power cleverly and maliciously. She lusts for Father Ralph and tries to tempt him to make love to her. His refusal—mainly because of his priestly vows but also because he finds her repulsive and pitiful—angers her and leads to her act of great malice. She makes a secret will in which she leaves her great estate to the Church, with the stipulations that Ralph is to administer it, that the Church must enable Ralph to advance, and that the Clearys always will have a home and work on Drogheda as well as generous individual incomes. She puts this will, along with an explanatory letter, into Ralph's hands, so that he has the choice of destroying it and leaving her previous will in effect. Then she dies, almost as if she wills her life to end.

Mary has cleverly foreseen that Ralph will be tempted by his ambition to produce the new will, thus cutting Meggie and her family out of their rightful inheritance but ensuring his own rise to power within the Church. She ensured that Meggie, whom she had seen as a rival for Ralph's affection, would be generously cared for, knowing that if Meggie were completely cut off, Ralph would destroy the new will. Mary understood exactly to what degree the warring sides of Ralph's nature had power over his behavior, and she played those varying impulses against each other with supreme cleverness. The will sets in motion the action of the novel to follow, motivating Ralph's actions and his feelings of guilt, just as Mary had foreseen. Of all the women in the novel, she is the only one who behaves with intentional malice. The others are short-sighted and when they make important choices, they all commit mistakes which cause great harm. But only Meggie's secrecy to Ralph about Dane's paternity can in any way be interpreted as intentionally vengeful. Meggie's malice is far less, however, because she truly loves both Ralph and Dane, and her intent is not solely to harm.

Much of Fee's experience had occurred before the action of the novel proper and is clarified only in flashback. Fee is presented as a dour, hardworking, long-suffering drudge, much loved by her husband and sons but unable to show them any affection. Life in New Zealand, where we first meet her, is a struggle, and her existence there is an unremitting round of toil. Only rarely does she show affection for her daughter, as when she gives Meggie a birthday gift of a doll in the novel's opening pages. Her oldest son, Frank, is her obvious favorite. Life on Drogheda in Australia eventually becomes easier for her, but her behavior towards her family changes little if at all. Thus when Mary Carson dies and the Clearys, despite losing control of the inheritance by the terms of Mary's will, are able to move to the big house, her behavior—her knowledge of finer things and her taste—comes as a surprise. She was from an old and prominent New Zealand family, and it is well into the novel that the reader learns what her children never learn in full, that her son, Frank, was the result of an affair with a married man whom she passionately loved. She had married Paddy to get away from her oppressive family, which was shamed by her and offered her to a man who otherwise would never have dared look at her.

This history explains some of her possessions as well as Paddy's adoration of her, her deep love for Frank, and her inability to admit affection for Paddy and her children by him. Sadly, it is only when he is suddenly killed that Fee realizes she loves Paddy, for whom she had always expressed respect and even affection, but never love. Her pride and her clinging to the past prevented her from valuing what she had in the present. In her later years, when she and Meggie come to understand each other, she mellows considerably. She finally understands that her obsessive love for her first lover was mistaken and kept her from realizing what she had in Paddy and in her family with him. Her guilt and wish to atone are deeply affecting.

Meggie lives a very different life from Fee's, but in some ironic ways she repeats Fee's experience and her mistakes. Her early years are spent in deprivation, but after Mary Carson's death, her life is much more comfortable. Drogheda, the leading station of the area, confers on her a status that must be similar to the one Fee had known while growing up in the very different society of New Zealand. Her mother never shows her any affection, and as the one girl in a family of men, she has no female comradeship and learns very little of what it means to be a woman. Her sex education, for example, is nonexistent. This point is poignantly made by a scene in which the adolescent Meggie, believing she is dying from cancer, must be taught about menstruation by Father Ralph. From Fee she seems to learn only that a woman's life is hard work and that nurturing babies is delightful. Her small brother Hal becomes her special charge and teaches her that she wants to have many babies. When he dies, she is devastated, for his loss removes from her the only creature she could care for and freely love.

Ralph's obvious affection for her from the moment they meet sets her apart and gives her a first taste of love. As naive as she is, and lacking any confidante to set her straight, she naturally centers her world around Ralph and eventually falls in love with him. Her ignorance of sex is paralleled by her lack of knowledge of what Ralph's priestly vocation means. She assumes he can simply stop being a priest and that he will do so when he realizes that they love each other. She clings to these illusions for a long time, and her misunderstandings lead to disaster. Having been cast aside, as she sees it, by Ralph, who has urged Fee to help her find a suitable husband, she marries Luke in haste and finds herself in a horrible situation. She hates Queensland, where he takes her, because its tropical, wet heat oppresses her. Luke abuses her psycholog-ically. Theirs is not really a marriage at all. Luke finds work for her as a domestic while he is off cutting sugar cane, in order, he says, to earn money to be put with her money to buy his own place. Luckily, the people with whom she lives and for whom she works are kind and take her into their hearts as well as their home.

What Meggie had wanted from the marriage is denied her. Her goals, which she could not get from Ralph but hoped to fulfill with Luke, were a home of her own and babies. She soon realizes that, whatever he ac-tually believes about himself, Luke is too much a wanderer ever to settle down and so she will never have a home with him. Babies also are impossible, for Luke does not want children and insists on using con-doms. The sex act is painful for her because Luke is totally insensitive. Only her pride keeps her from leaving Luke and returning to Drogheda. When she learns about Luke's use of condoms, she tricks him into an act of unprotected sex and finally succeeds in becoming pregnant. After a hard pregnancy, she delivers her daughter, Justine, who is a difficult child. Her employer, deeply concerned for her well-being and promising to care for Justine, sends her off alone for a holiday on Matlock Island, usually a honeymoon resort but currently nearly deserted. Ralph comes to Matlock, and their idyllic and rapturous meeting leads to the consum-mation of their love and to Meggie's second pregnancy.

Meggie's love for babies and her yearning to have them motivate much of her action. Her other prime motivations are her pride and, at times, her naiveté. Her love for Ralph and her naiveté make her unable to understand and then unwilling to accept that his priestly vocation and vows make their love for each other impossible. She marries Luke partly from anger at Ralph, partly from pride, partly to get the babies she longs for, and partly because he reminds her physically of Ralph. Their marriage is doomed from the beginning because they have no love for each other and have both gone into it for poor reasons. Luke's responsibility for the marriage's failure is obvious—he is totally selfish and shows absolutely no understanding or affection for Meggie—but her own guilt is no less real. She uses him for her own purposes—escape, babies—just as much as he uses her. She is always headstrong. Her pride carries her into a disastrous marriage, and her pride keeps her from leaving Luke and returning home long after she knows the marriage has no chance to bring her any sort of fulfillment. After her idyll with Ralph, Meggie shows her most decisive side and behaves with determination. She resolves that Ralph will never know he has fathered a child, and she tricks Luke into one last act of sexual intercourse, so he will think the child is his, before she returns home permanently to Drogheda, where her son Dane is born.

At this point, Meggie has achieved those goals which seem possible and has given up or compromised on those which do not. She has given up the hope of any permanent relationship with Ralph, but she has the knowledge that his son is hers to mold and control. If she does not have a home of her own, she has Drogheda and an important place there with strenuous outside work to do she enjoys.

The rest of the novel, as far as Meggie is concerned, is principally the story of her learning that she cannot control Dane any more than she could Ralph. Like Ralph, he escapes her, and his escape comes about, ironically, because he carries within himself all the best side of Ralph, all that which made Ralph also turn away from her. She rebels in anger when he tells her he wishes to become a priest, and she refuses to go to Rome for his ordination. She maintains her secrecy about Dane's parentage until, in desperate anger after his death, she explodes at Ralph when she forces him to help her find Dane's body, buried in an unmarked grave in Crete, and bring it back for interment at Drogheda. Only when it is too late for Ralph to do anything about his fatherhood does she reveal it and then only in anger. This behavior indicates how little she has learned from all her experience, all her anguish. Her often misdirected longings for excitement and, especially, for love and babies had led mainly to pain.

That she does finally learn something is revealed in the later pages of the novel, when she and Fee talk about their pasts and when she renounces her attempts to control her remaining child, Justine. She was on the verge of winning a struggle over Justine's future, of bringing her daughter back to Drogheda permanently. Rainer, Justine's German lover, gives Meggie a choice rather like the one Mary Carson had given Ralph so many years ago, a choice in which acting for the best interests of the one she loved would also destroy her own hopes. Unlike Ralph, she selects the nobler choice, freeing Justine to live her own life and avoid the mistakes of her mother and grandmother.

Justine, the third generation of these women, is from the beginning very much her own person. A difficult baby, she grows into a difficult child and becomes a torment to Meggie, who finds herself unable to love the baby as she expected to do. Justine seems less her own baby, less lovable, than had her brother Hal, for whom she had so lovingly cared years before. It is ironic that, in some respects, Justine repeats her own experience, for just as Meggie had cared for Hal and been more his mother than Fee, so Justine cares for the baby Dane and sees him as her great treasure. Justine, like Meggie, feels unloved by her mother. Quite unlike Meggie, however, Justine never considers herself a domestic creature. Marriage and babies are not the great goal of her life. Her ambition is to become an actress. If pride is a distinguishing characteristic of Meggie's, then independence is Justine's parallel characteristic.

Justine and Dane always have a particularly close bond, starting in their early childhood when Justine mothers him. When he goes to Rome to enter seminary, Justine goes to London to study acting, so that she can be close enough to him to spend holidays with him. After his ordination, she first agrees to accompany him on a holiday trip to Greece before he goes to visit Meggie on Drogheda. She backs out of the holiday trip, however, because she is given a chance at a leading role on the London stage, and when his holiday ends in his tragic death, she blames herself. Her ambition, she feels, led her to desert her brother, and if she had not done so, he would have lived. Guilt is an important motivation for the rest of her behavior.

That guilt leads Justine to refuse marriage to Rainer and to decide to give up the acting career which now seems unfulfilling in light of the tragedy of her brother's death. She had long held Rainer off, refusing to commit herself to him, though for most of their bumpy courtship her reasons had mainly involved her immersion in her career. Eventually, her choice is formulated as a decision between family and Drogheda, on the one hand, and love and career, on the other, because Rainer will encourage her to continue on the stage. Her deep, if wrongheaded, guilt over Dane's death pushes her back toward Drogheda and Meggie, and her prospects there seem limited to a conventional marriage with a member of another prominent sheep-raising family, exactly the kind of life she had rejected when she went to London in the first place. When Meggie, having been encouraged by Fee, writes to Justine to tell her not to come home but rather to marry her German lover, all three women finally are freed from the progression of obsessive love and guilt that has stifled the lives of the two older ones. Justine, then, though less interesting and less successfully characterized than either Fee or Meggie, is necessary to bring to a conclusion the cycle of pain of three generations of Cleary women.

Many of the male characters in *The Thorn Birds* have interesting stories, and a number of them are effectively and believably characterized. All of them, even Ralph de Bricassart, who became the central figure of the television miniseries (perhaps because the actor playing him had the biggest name), are subsidiary to the three Cleary women. Their stories are included to motivate or explain the motivations of Fee, Meggie, and, to a lesser extent, Justine. The men may be examined, then, in relationship to the three women. For Fee, there are her husband, Paddy, and her eldest son, Frank. For Meggie, the most important men are Ralph de Bricassart, Luke O'Neill, and Dane. And finally for Justine, in addition to Dane, there is Rainer Moerling Hartheim.

As first introduced, Paddy Cleary seems a feckless Irish sheep shearer who has not managed to succeed well enough in New Zealand to support his large and growing family adequately and who is so tired from his labors that he has little energy to express affection for his wife or children. That he does not know how to express his love for his children is clear, but his comradeship with his sons, all except the eldest, Frank, seems to balance that shortcoming. With his daughter Meggie, however, he seems to lack the ability to relate at all. His wife he adores, and it is only when he and Frank have an argument and he blurts out the fact of Frank's birth out of wedlock that some of the complexities of the family relationships are clarified. Paddy resents Frank, the son of the lover Fee has never forgotten, and he knows that her love for Frank stands in the way of her loving him and their children. But he also knows that if it had not been for Frank's birth, he would never have had a chance to marry her. He tries to do his best, but he can never feel the same affection for Frank as he does for his own sons, and thus there is always a division in the family—understood only by Paddy and Fee—about which Fee refuses to do anything.

Paddy is a good man, a hard worker, and a devoted husband and father. As life becomes easier for the family, after Mary's death, when they move to the big house and have not only practical control of the station but also individual and generous incomes, he tries to pamper Fee, attempting to atone to her for all her years of deprivation and toil. His death—which also causes the death of one of his sons—is sudden and dramatic, an expression of the harsh cruelty of the land. After years of drought, when the trees are at their driest, a brush fire sweeps across Drogheda, catching Paddy alone and killing him horribly. In the search mounted for him, when rain mercifully puts out the fire, his son Stuart finds his body, shoots his rifle to signal his discovery, is charged by a crazed wild boar, and, lacking time to reload his rifle, is killed. Paddy's death removes from the plot a male character who no longer has a role to play in the action, illustrates again the harshness of the land, teaches Fee that she really did love Paddy, and causes her great grief and guilt and a desire to atone. It also leads to a passionate kiss between Ralph and Meggie when he tries to comfort her, a first revelation to the two of them of their continuing though impossible love for each other.

Frank seems a minor character, but his story forms a distinct subplot and serves a number of functions for the more important female characters, especially for Fee. His very existence, of course, motivates the socially unequal marriage of Paddy to Fee and helps to explain the emotional poverty of the Cleary family. It adds to Fee's suffering. But taken separately it also is a tale of pain and suffering which is complete in itself. From the beginning of the novel, Frank is complex. Meggie's one kind and loving brother, Frank repeatedly comforts her and attempts to fix her sorrows. He rescues the doll her other brothers are thoughtlessly destroying in the novel's opening pages. It is to him that she turns for nurturing until Father de Bricassart comes into her life. Frank always feels himself an outcast within the family, without knowing why, and there is a strain of rage and destructiveness within him. Knowing nothing of his irregular birth, he somehow feels that he owned his mother first, that he has something with her that the others lack.

Feeling alien from the family, he repeatedly tries to escape. A series of highly dramatic scenes lead up to his final leaving. He had always been a good fighter, and the anger that is deeply embedded in his character, but which he does not understand, expresses itself in the boxing ring. He accepts the challenge of a traveling troupe of boxers and wins twenty pounds by fighting several of the professionals, including their champion. Meggie and Ralph see him fight and Meggie is frightened and horrified, but Frank finds release in letting his anger come out against his opponent. Paddy and Frank, both already emotionally over-wrought, confront each other and in their verbal battle, Paddy lets slip the fact that Frank is not his own son. After learning about his true parentage, Frank joins the troupe of boxers, leaving a void in the lives of Fee and Meggie.

Frank's disappearance seems to put an end to his membership in the family. However, some years later, just as life is beginning to get easier for the Clearys and Fee is beginning to show some happiness, they learn accidentally that Frank has received a life sentence for murder. A fight in a bar had escalated into a brutal beating of his opponent, whom he had killed by repeated blows and kicks. Again Frank's rage had ex-pressed itself violently, and the only way in which he seems to show any regret is in his wish that his mother not be told. After about thirty years, he is paroled and comes home to Drogheda, a broken man who has had all the anger taken from him. He says little and tends the Drogh-eda gardens, seeming to find some sort of peace there.

Frank's history is filled with pathos, and in creating him McCullough has explained much of Fee's behavior and the mistakes she makes. But she has also told the story of a tragic life of interest in itself and set up parallels with her main characters. Frank's conception is no less irregular and no less the result of passion than is Dane's. Meggie no less than Fee took conscious action to give her son a name: Fee married Paddy and Meggie briefly returned to Luke. Fee is more fortunate than Meggie in her husband, but both women are unable to love the men whom they marry. Frank is very unlike Dane in character and personality. The gentle side of Frank, his nurturing and helping his mother and sister, are not unlike Dane's gentleness. Dane, however, has none of the anger that destroys Frank.

The three men who affect Meggie's life contrast with each other in a variety of ways. Central to Meggie's story, of course, is her obsessive and passionate love for Father Ralph de Bricassart. Ralph is so fully and complexly depicted that his character sometimes seems to take over the novel. McCullough has said that he was intended to play a minor role. However, she was "aware I didn't have a dominant male lead. The min-ute the priest walked into the book I said, 'Ah ha, this is it! This is the male character I've lacked!'" (Cassill 36). In fact, only a few—mostly mi-nor—changes in plot and presentation turned Ralph into the central character in the television miniseries (doubtless because Richard Cham-berlain, the actor who played the part, was the biggest star).

Ralph is a man in deep conflict with himself. A Roman Catholic priest, he is sent from his native Ireland to Gillanbone, the village nearest Drogheda, before the Clearys arrive. Before his part in the action begins, he has already decided that the priestly side of him will dominate. He loves God deeply. He is also ambitious, with a powerful desire to rise within the Church, a goal that seems unlikely of fulfillment so long as he is buried in that remote place. Warring with the priestly and spiritual side of his nature is his human side. The narrative often frames the conflict as between the priest and the man: a struggle between religious faith and worldly pleasure, between priestly humility and ambition, between the chastity of his priestly vows and his deep desire for sexual fulfillment with Meggie. All these struggles, even the strange power of his interest in the still childish Meggie, are recognized by Mary Carson, enabling her to tempt him cleverly through her will, a temptation she knows he will be unable to resist.

In becoming a priest, Ralph had taken the three vows of obedience, chastity, and poverty. That he broke the vow of obedience while in Ireland is hinted at, but that vow is not really significant to the novel. He breaks the other two vows within the plot. The vow of poverty is broken in principle when he accepts the terms of Mary Carson's will. Though her estate becomes the property of the Church, he has control over it as its administrator. So, while legally he does not possess great wealth, he has the power given by those riches. And his being instrumental in enriching the Church by the sum of thirteen million pounds brings much favorable attention to him from the Church hierarchy, which would have occurred even if Mary Carson had not stipulated in the will that her bequest to the Church was valid only if the Church recognize Ralph's worth. When he chooses to present the will, Ralph breaks his vow of poverty by selling Meggie's birthright for, as he himself puts it, "thirteen million pieces of silver" (154). Of course what tempts him is less the money itself than the power conferred on him by that money, as well as the chance to rise to become a cardinal, a prince of the Church. Ambition is his expression of the greed which the vow of poverty is intended to destroy. In making that central choice of the novel, Ralph expresses the human side of his personality, the "man" within him, even while, ironically, he guarantees his rise to power within the Church. And that rise is regular and methodical, and he does eventually, as Mary and he had separately foreseen, become Cardinal de Bricassart.

The vow of chastity is one he long struggles with, repeatedly pushing Meggie aside. She repeatedly tempts him, partly from her first naive belief that he can stop being a priest and partly from the depths of her obsessive love. She deeply resents the Church's requirement for the celibacy of priests and blames the Church for ruining her life, for making her marry Luke because she could not marry Ralph. Meggie's motives are no less mixed than are Ralph's, and their idyll, when it comes on Matlock Island, is doomed to be only a brief encounter. In fact, Ralph does not consciously intend to do anything more than see Meggie for what might be a last time when he joins her there. He pledges that he will not "involve Meggie in anything which might endanger her immortal soul" (310), but a sudden realization of the depth of his passion for her as an adult woman, not the child he had unconsciously still seen her as, leads to his taking her. Their passionate and tender interlude represents her temporary victory over the priest in him and his surrender to what she had called his "manhood," which the Church did not want but would not allow her to have.

A brief scene, only about a page in length, sets up Ralph's conflict over his passion for Meggie. Long before their love is consummated, he is given the assignment of telling a young priest of his punishment for an affair with a woman he loves deeply. Ralph is firm and clear as he lectures the unnamed young priest on his sin in breaking his vow of chastity and on the shame he has brought on himself and on the Church. More painful is the punishment he metes out: the young priest is exiled immediately to a remote parish with no chance to say goodbye to the young woman he loves. Furthermore, he is told that he will be closely watched to ensure he make no attempt to contact her. She will never know where he has gone. No mention is made of Meggie in this scene, nor are Ralph's feelings indicated. But the application to his own situation, to his yearning for young Meggie, is clear. The scene has the function of reinforcing for the reader the full import of Ralph's vocation and position in the Church and the impossibility of his ever becoming free to marry.

Repeatedly Ralph rationalizes the beauty of his love for Meggie. He associates her with roses (which she once reminds him have thorns but which to him mean only beauty and sweetness). He also thinks of her and their relationship as being somehow sacramental. The sacraments may be defined as tangible symbols of spiritual realities. To Ralph, Meggie sometimes seems a human representation of love, and to him she brings emotional, even spiritual, release. Thus in her he tries to unify the man and the priest and reconcile the struggle within himself. He never succeeds in doing so.

Following the idyllic period with Meggie on Matlock Island, Ralph's role in the novel becomes less prominent. In Rome, his rise in the Church continues, and he loves and accepts Dane both for the qualities he sees within the young man he does not know is his son and for the sake of Meggie, Dane's mother. By enabling Dane's entrance into the priesthood and by finding and inspiring the young German soldier who later becomes Justine's lover, he helps to move the plot forward. But he is no longer so near the center of the action.

Luke, Meggie's husband, is, after Mary Carson, the most unlikable character in the novel. He is totally centered on self and is lacking in self-awareness. A hard worker, he is ambitious, thinking that his goal is to become the owner of the best sheep station in Queensland. In order to achieve that goal, he labors at backbreaking jobs (first sheep shearing and then cane cutting), and he marries Meggie for her money. Meggie is not the first heiress to whom he had paid court, and his disappointment in learning the Clearys only managed and did not own Drogheda is only partly overcome by his discovery of her generous income. He is quite unscrupulous and intentional in his goals for their marriage. That Meggie is attractive and lively is a bonus but not necessary. After marriage, he continues his single-minded pursuit of his goal. He takes Meggie on a miserable journey to Queensland and hires himself out to a traveling crew, requiring his living with the other cutters. He finds a job for her as a housemaid, giving her a place to live rent free and enabling her to bring in some small additional income. He never consults her about her wishes in the matter.

Eventually Meggie realizes that Luke has become obsessed with the work itself and that he enjoys his life with the men. Like Ralph, he has no place in his life for a woman, a home, or babies. Like Ralph, she realizes, he is ambitious, and his ambition excludes her. Ralph and Luke represents opposites in some regards. One is gentle and sensitive and introspective, while the other is brutal and selfish and unaware. But they resemble each other physically, and that similarity in appearance masks deeper and more important likenesses. Neither is able to give Meggie what she requires because of deep internal needs which are at odds with her yearnings. Each does, however, without intending to do so, give her a child. Luke refuses to have anything to do with Justine, and Ralph does not know that Dane is his son until after Dane has drowned. Ralph represents what she yearns for until after Dane's birth, when she finally recenters her life on her children and Drogheda. Luke represents her great mistake, made because Ralph had cast her off, because he reminded her of Ralph, and because she mistakenly thought that, through him, she could achieve the goals that Ralph denied her.

The third important man in Meggie's life is Dane, who also is very important for the development of Justine. From the beginning, he is like his father without Ralph's internal conflict. For him the priestly requirements of poverty, chastity, and obedience seem to be natural. Meggie is angry at his decision to become a priest, for she sees that choice as Ralph's ultimate revenge on her. Dane will not, as she had hoped, continue the line of Cleary descendants at Drogheda. All her hatred of the Church for having cheated her of Ralph returns when Dane decides, unknowingly, to follow his father into the priestly vocation.

Dane is recognized by everyone as special. When he goes to Rome, Ralph and his associates at the Vatican are drawn to him immediately, loving what Ralph thinks of as his beautiful soul. His progress through his seminary training seems untroubled, and he prays naturally and fervently. If there is a flaw, as he sees himself, it is that he has not suffered and thus cannot be the perfect priest others expect. His death, apparently a heart attack caused by overexertion in rescuing a potential drowning victim, brings him brief but acute pain. He struggles against death, briefly cries out against it, and then accepts the pain as sent from God. Thinking that his pain is like that which Christ felt on the cross, he rejoices that this suffering is brief, and he dies in an ecstasy of love for God. His prayers for suffering have been answered, and he is, in death, the perfect priest. Perhaps he had to die, so soon after his ordination, simply because he had achieved a kind of perfection that cannot survive in this world. At any rate, unlike Ralph, sometimes considered a perfect priest, Dane fulfills the promise others had seen in him.

The last of the male characters of any real significance is Rainer Moerling Hartheim, friend and protégé of Ralph and lover of Justine. During World War II, Ralph discovers Rainer in Saint Peter's, huddled under Michelangelo's *Pietè*. A young and frightened German soldier, opposed to the Nazis, he is afraid of being sent to the Russian front. A foundling who had chosen his own name, he fears he might be thought to be Jewish because he has no knowledge of his parentage. Ralph, who is drawn to him, promises to pray for him. And that is the end of their brief initial encounter.

Rainer is established in this brief episode as free from the influence of the past, unlike the women characters or Ralph. Just as he invents his own name, so he creates himself. He reenters the novel much later, after the war, when he has already become a successful businessman and politician. Like Luke, he had married for money, with no concern for the well-being or needs of his wife. His first wife, who was older than he, was the widow of a wealthy industrialist. Rainer used her wealth to begin his own business career and divorced her when he no longer had any need of her. Unlike Luke and like Ralph, however, he at least has some sense of shame for his actions, and McCullough explicitly points out the latter similarity: "Like Ralph de Bricassart he understood he did wrong even as he did it. Not that his awareness of the evil in him stopped him for a second, only that he paid for his material advancement in pain and self-torment" (451). He learns from his mistakes, partly because of the good influence on him of Ralph, with whom he establishes a friendship after the war. McCullough shows little of his "pain and self-torment," but she does dramatize the maturity and sensitivity which he develops as a result of his self-awareness.

He falls in love with Justine but recognizes her inability to love, to give herself to another. Patiently, he dose not rush her or force her to make choices she is unwilling or unable to make. McCullough comments that, because of this requirement for the character, he "had to be a German because he had to be prepared to wait ten years for a woman." The qualities of "romanticism and hard-headedness," which she imputes to the Germans as a nationality along with being "tremendously romantic, very disciplined and patient" (Cassill 36), sum up her characterization of Rainer.

Unlike other male characters, Rainer learns from his mistakes. Feeling regret for his treatment of his first wife (though not sorrow at having profited from the relationship), he tries to accomplish what is best for Justine and to free her to make her own choices. He challenges Meggie to help Justine see that her best future is with him even though Meggie would have to give up Justine, against her own best interest. This challenge is oddly reminiscent of the choice Mary Carson placed before Ralph years ago, with the crucial difference that Mary Carson intended Ralph to give in to his temptation while Rainer hopes Meggie will be able to give Justine her freedom. His sensitivity and patience are rewarded, and Justine is finally able to overcome her unwarranted guilt and decide to make her life with him.

STYLE, IMAGES, AND SYMBOLS

McCullough has never been known as a stylist, that is for having a facility with language or for using images in a particularly effective way. *The Thorn Birds* was severely criticized by reviewers, in fact, for a plodding and ungraceful style which included unbelievable dialogue. It is agreed that her talent is that of a storyteller who can make her readers care about her characters and what happens to them, not that of one who creates a narrative with a graceful texture which enhances the telling. *The Thorn Birds* nevertheless contains some useful images which serve particular functions in the presentation of the novel's materials. Several are especially helpful in depicting characters and relationships. The most important one grows from the novel's title, which states its central theme.

One important image is used by Ralph for Mary Carson. Repeatedly he thinks of her as a spider, an image which captures her malice and her conscious weaving a web of evil as well as his emotional rejection of her as a woman, the rejection that ironically increases her desire to punish him. Like a spider, she intentionally ensnares her prey and destroys it. Her will and the accompanying letter challenging Ralph to do the right thing and destroy the will create her cleverest, most destructive web. The repeated use of the spider image, always in Ralph's thoughts, reveals his awareness of her true nature even as it stresses her actual malice and cruelty.

In contrast to Ralph's persistent vision of Mary Carson as a spider is his repeated view of Meggie as "a sacrament." This way of seeing her illustrates his need to define things in religious terms. He cannot admit his love for a completely human person but must translate that loved object into spiritual language. One brief scene, in which Ralph twice thinks of her in this language, will illustrate. Long after their liaison on Matlock Island, they briefly renew their physical relationship at Drogheda. As they kiss, his thoughts are indirectly conveyed. He is aware of "that mouth alive under his, not a dream, so long wanted, so long. A different kind of sacrament, dark like the earth, having nothing to do with the sky" (388). And a few pages later, his thoughts compare her with the actual sacrament of the mass: "Tomorrow morning I'll say Mass," he thinks. "But that's tomorrow morning.... There is still the night, and Meggie.... She, too, is a sacrament" (394).

In the sacrament of the Mass, the bread and wine become the body and blood of Christ, with whom the worshipper is united in the act of partaking of the elements. Ralph's association of the Mass with Meggie suggests that she symbolizes something spiritual for him, with which he is united in the sexual act. Perhaps he is here attempting to join his physical and spiritual sides, the man and the priest in him. That he is rationalizing about his passion for her is clear, and his making her into an abstraction is a kind of idealization and romanticization which contrasts with her earthy need of him.

More important for the novel as a whole is the image of roses, especially the "dusky, pale pinkish grey, the color that in those days was called ashes of roses" (134). When the Clearys first arrive at Drogheda, the masses of rosebushes around the homestead help make it seem like the lush, green New Zealand they have left, so unlike dusty, dry New South Wales. Throughout the novel, the roses are repeatedly mentioned, often in association with Meggie. Her first party dress, when she is sixteen, is in the ashes of roses shade, and she is particularly lovely in it. Ralph is torn by conflicting feelings, pride in her beauty and sorrow that she is growing up. Memories of that party and that dress are referred to throughout the novel, so that the moment becomes a special one and is seen as one which changed their relationship from that of a mature man and a child to that between two adults. It is also the color she is wearing when they briefly renew their affair after many years of separation. Meggie becomes Ralph's rose. In a moment of renunciation after Paddy's death, when he thinks he is leaving forever, Ralph urges Fee to help Meggie find some suitable young man to marry. Meggie, saying farewell, gives Ralph a rose, described as "pale, pinkish-gray" and thus similar in shade to "ashes of roses" (210). He presses it in his missal and it becomes his romantic memento of Meggie. Later he tells her about the rose in his missal and calls her his rose, expecting these tender words to bring her joy. Instead, she explodes angrily at him and points out his romanticism, which she considers foolish. She tells him he does not know what love is really about, and she reminds him that roses have thorns, a line which connects this rose imagery to the thorns of the novel's title.

Another association, suggested by Meggie, occurs later. When Dane tells her he wishes to become a priest, she is shocked and horrified. She sees God as winning the battle she has been carrying on against Him all her life. In taking Dane from her, He is taking away her victory over Ralph. Now she connects the name of the color that had meant so much to her to the phrase associated with death and funerals. "Ashes of roses," she gasps and bursts into blasphemy.

"And I didn't understand. . . . Ashes thou wert, unto ashes return. To the Church thou belongest, to the Church thou shalt
be given. . . . God rot God, I say! God the sod! The utmost
Enemy of women, that's what God is!" (425).

The beautiful flower, associated with her home and with her love as well
as her anger, now becomes connected to her great loss. And when Dane
is buried, his casket is covered with roses, associating the flowers again
with pain and grief.

Roses are a trite symbol for love, but the symbol is inverted in *The
Thorn Birds*. In associating roses with Drogheda, McCullough used them
rather conventionally. The use of ashes of roses continued that conventional usage, but within the name that color already contains a paradox.
To become ashes, the roses must burn. They must go through fire in
order to create the beauty of the color. Through suffering and pain,
beauty is created. This motif connects obviously with the meaning of the
novel's title, and McCullough uses the shifting meaning of roses and
ashes of roses to convey her central theme.

The novel's title is explained by an epigraph placed before its opening.
It summarizes a Celtic legend of a bird which searches all its life for a
thorn on which it may impale itself. That act, which kills it, enables it to
sing so beautifully that its song is the loveliest thing in the world. The
moral is, we are told, that "the best is only bought at the cost of great
pain." The title is referred to only occasionally in the course of the novel.
In a moment of acceptance, Meggie explains to Ralph what she has
learned:

"Each of us has something within us which won't be denied,
even if it makes us scream aloud to die. . . . Like the old Celtic
legend of the bird with the thorn in its breast, singing its heart
out and dying. Because it has to, it's driven to. We can know
what we do wrong even before we do it, but self-knowledge
can't affect or change the outcome, can it? Everyone singing
his own little song, convinced it's the most wonderful song
the world has ever heard. . . . We create our own thorns, and
never stop to count the cost. All we can do is suffer the pain,
and tell ourselves it was well worth it." (390)

The novel closes in Meggie's thoughts, when she receives a cable telling her of Justine's marriage to Rainer. She smells the perfume of the

roses in the Drogheda garden and thinks of its beauty but also of its ending. The ending of the Clearys and their descendants on Drogheda is now certain, and she sees that as the conclusion of a cycle. She accepts her own responsibility for its happening, but she regrets nothing. Then, in the book's final paragraph, the point of view becomes less clear. Whether Meggie is still meditating on the meaning of her life or whether the author is commenting on the meaning of her story is ambiguous. That final paragraph refers again to the legend of the thorn bird, ecstatic in the beauty of its song but unaware of its dying, and ends by universalizing its message: "But we, when we put the thorns in our breasts, we know. We understand. And still we do it. Still we do it" (530).

THEMATIC ISSUES

All fiction, whether intentionally on the part of the author or not, expresses themes or abstract ideas. *The Thorn Birds,* which is not particularly theme driven, relies on characters and story for its interest and its achievement of a sense of deeper meaning through the use of images and symbols. Among the themes which are particularly obvious are the effects of repressive methods of child-rearing and the difficulties of life for members of the working classes in the early years of this century in New Zealand and Australia. Changes in life on Australian sheep stations over the period from World War I to the late 1960s are illustrated. Irish Catholicism and the hierarchy of the Roman Catholic Church are depicted critically. Most of these themes are inherent in the historical materials used in the novel and relate to the book as an example of the multigenerational family saga. They create a context for the characters and relationships and for the central theme of suffering.

That central notion examined in *The Thorn Birds* is pointed out in the Celtic legend of the title. All the major characters suffer, and for each there is some repayment though frequently not enough. For Fee, the thwarted love for her first lover brings her Frank, who is taken from her, and Paddy, whom she does not realize she loves until it is too late. Meggie's obsession with Ralph brings a few moments of rapture and the gift of Dane, who is also taken from her—first by the Church and then by his untimely death. Meggie and Justine both feel unworthy because of their mothers' inability or refusal to show them any love. For Justine, there is guilt for being unable to love and for, she thinks, causing her brother's death. The men suffer, too. Paddy loves Fee desperately and never knows she cares at all for him. Frank is torn by his rage and his devoted love for the mother he thinks is being abused by her husband. His ultimate suffering, of course, occurs off stage, in the long imprisonment that breaks his spirit. Ralph is torn between his two sides, his love for God and the Church and his passion for Meggie. Only Luke and Dane do not truly suffer: Luke is not sensitive enough, and Dane is too good. Dane, in fact, prays for the suffering that will enable him to become the perfect priest, and his prayers are answered by the brief physical pain he endures at his death.

Related to the theme of suffering is that of love and lust as destructive forces. Love leads to the suffering of Fee and Meggie and causes Ralph to break his vow of chastity. Lust impels Mary Carson to create the cruel choice Ralph must make. By making him decide whether to present the will leaving her fortune to the Church (but in his control), she forces him to choose between his integrity and his love for Meggie, on the one hand, and his ambition to rise in the Church, on the other. Love becomes lust in the lives of these characters when it is not joined by true concern for the one loved. Selfish love repeatedly leads individual characters to behave in ways that damage others. Fee, obsessed with her first lover and with his son, withholds herself from her loving second husband and her children by him. In so doing she deprives herself as well as Paddy and Meggie of joy and support. Meggie, unable to think of anyone except Ralph, marries Luke, who is totally unsuited for her; withholds herself from her daughter, as Fee had withheld herself from Meggie; and separates Ralph and Dane from any possibility of being father and son. Ralph teases Meggie by refusing her and yet by returning repeatedly to her. Only Rainer finally loves unselfishly, considering Justine's needs as much as he considers his own. Thus it is through his wisdom that he and Justine are able to bring closure to the cycle of thwarted love which had followed three generations of Cleary women.

Another aspect of the theme of love is connected to ambition and the idea of the perfect priest. Both Ralph and Dane are referred to as perfect priests, but this reference is always ironic in relationship to Ralph. He seems to be the perfect priest, for he does all the external things well and makes an outwardly ideal impression. He is effective in ministering to others, but his rise in the Church removes him from the priestly functions of caring for and comforting ordinary human souls. His sexual involvement with Meggie is only the most dramatic illustration of the flaws that make him a very imperfect priest in the reality which underlies his appearance. Ralph's perfection is outward. Dane's, on the other hand, is inward and real. Dane is whole hearted and whole souled in a way that Ralph, tormented with internal conflict, can never be. A very new priest, just ordained, he gives his life to save another and, in suffering and dying, proves that he represents the reality of the perfect priest. Ironically, it is in the moment of achieving that perfection, through the suffering which he knew he had lacked, that he must die. Perhaps perfection in priests is no more possible in this imperfect world than is perfection in anything else. Just as the color ashes of roses represents a joining of suffering and beauty, so here perfection joins with death.

A FEMINIST READING OF *THE THORN BIRDS*

Feminist criticism is based on feminism, a social movement related to the struggle of women to achieve complete equality. In actuality, it is probably better to speak of "feminisms," using the plural, for there are many varieties of feminism, stressing various goals and using various methods. Many radical feminists urge the destruction of the present social structure, which gives most power and authority to men; other feminists believe in working for a gradual change within the system. Feminists have undertaken a variety of causes, among which are the adoption of the Equal Rights Amendment (which failed after a long and bitter struggle), the accomplishment of equal pay for equal or equivalent work, the protection of women and their children from abuse by husbands and other men, equal access to education and jobs and professional advancement, and many other goals.

Feminist writers tend to present their ideas in fiction in two basic ways. One is to show what is wrong and the other is exemplify what is more desirable. One who uses the first method might depict women who are traditional in their attitudes (who desire only to marry and have children and live a life of domesticity). Such a writer might then show how those attitudes may lead to disaster (the seemingly perfect marriage ending in divorce or the death of the husband, perhaps), leaving the woman unable to support and care for herself and her children because she has no training or skills. Domesticity may be shown to be a trap, not a "happy ending." A writer who uses the second method might create strong women who succeed despite all the obstacles a patriarchal society (that is, one run by and for men) can put in their way. Independence, rather than reliance on a male, will be shown as desirable. Both writers would have the same goal of helping readers focus on the needs of women and showing them how women can live effective and fulfilled lives. Feminist writers also examine issues and problems facing women, such as poverty, abuse, discrimination based on gender, and so on. They dramatize the lives of female characters facing those issues. They illustrate attitudes toward women of both women and men. Definitions of "femininity" and what the ideal woman should be like may also be discussed.

Feminist critics look at writings by feminist and nonfeminist writers in different ways. They assume that women are as important, talented, and interesting as men and point out that this assumption is not universal. They point out how literature examines the ways in which women have been exploited and suppressed. Such critics point out social conditions, prejudices, inimical legal provisions, and many other ways in which women have not been treated equally with men in literature. Feminist critics also look at the work of women writers, trying to ensure that the work of these writers is treated fairly and not dismissed simply because of their female authorship. These critics point out issues or themes of particular importance to women and study the ways in which female characters are depicted. Feminist approaches sometimes lead critics to examine the presentation of male characters and themes, for these often affect female characters and themes as well.

In reading *The Thorn Birds* as a feminist, one immediately recognizes the emphasis within the plot and characterization of this novel on women as being born to suffer. The parallel experiences of three generations of Cleary women illustrate the pain that comes to women because they love and the guilt and need for atonement that follow obsessive love for men who do not really need them. Fee suffers all her life as a result of her youthful love for a prominent, married politician. She showers all her love on her son by that man and cheats both the husband, who truly does love her, and her other children, especially her daughter. After the death of her husband and one of their sons, she realizes that she deeply loved them both and finds herself unable to love her daughter because her daughter is a reminder of her own errors, someone who will repeat her own mistakes and relive her own suffering. She tries not to think of Meggie as any different from her sons (209). Meggie repeats Fee's rejection of her, finding herself unable to love Justine as she dotes on her son Dane. The lot of women is to love and suffer—or so it seems until the end of the novel, when Justine finally overcomes her guilt and sense of unworthiness and is able to give herself to Rainer.

The feminist critic might argue that McCullough has stacked the decks.

She has presented Fee and Meggie with men who are not available—Fee's lover is already being married, and Meggie's is married to the Church. Justine is more fortunate in finding Rainer, who not only is available but is willing to wait patiently for her to be ready for him. As Fee and Meggie eventually realize, they have caused much of their own suffering, and Meggie comes to believe that her few moments of ecstasy and her motherhood of Dane made the suffering worthwhile. Ironically, when Fee and Meggie finally come to an understanding late in the novel, Fee tells Meggie that she enjoys her because they are equals, though she never enjoyed her sons in that same way (377). Perhaps their very sharing of the burdens of womanhood is what enables them to empathize with and enjoy each other.

The novel is based on patriarchal assumptions and set in a strongly patriarchal society. Patriarchy, literally "rule by the fathers," is involved whenever men have power over women, whether that power be exercised through the legal system, through the force of custom, or through internalized acceptance by women of their own inferiority. Luke's assumption that Meggie's money will become his personal property when they marry, an assumption that he baldly expresses to her and which she accepts unquestioningly, illustrates the power of patriarchal thinking. Meggie is a very feminine woman in the traditional sense—having her own home and babies is the central goal of her life. Domesticity is what she longs for and can never have with Ralph. Ralph thinks of her ability to bear burdens as being particularly "womanly," one of the things he especially loves in her (313). All these details underscore the patriarchal nature of the society and reveal the assumptions of the characters that women are lesser beings than men, born to suffer and to support the efforts of their men.

In this patriarchal world, relationships between men become important, and McCullough illustrates male bonding in three different contexts: within the Cleary family, among male laborers, and in the Roman Catholic hierarchy. With the partial exception of the Cleary family, these are three different worlds in which women have no place and from which they are consciously and intentionally excluded. Within the family, there are a number of sons and only one daughter. The carrying on of the Cleary name to the next generation should have been assured, and yet Meggie is the only member of the second generation of the family to marry or to have children. The sons elect to remain part of the family on the homestead, and they form no meaningful relationships outside the family. They never become involved with women, seemingly unable or uninterested in romantic or sexual connections. Frank leaves home, but the result is his commission of a murder, his long prison sentence, and his return to his family a broken man. The youngest sons, twins, who serve together in World War II, are so close to each other that there is no room for anyone else in their lives. When one is wounded in such a way that his sexual function is destroyed, little is actually lost—the permanent effects of the wound seem more symbolic than practical. The Cleary men are perhaps not very highly sexed. Or perhaps they are so close to each other that they have no need of sex or of women.

Luke is less aware of his male bonding than are Meggie's brothers. He thinks he wants to achieve his own place, but in fact he becomes a part of a male culture which has no need of women and little interest in them (except as sex objects) when he joins the crew of cane cutters. When he enters the story, he is part of a group of sheep shearers who travel about the stations hiring out as needed. That status seems a temporary expedient but turns out to represent the sort of life he demands. With his "mate" (an Australian slang term for "close male friend" but particularly appropriate in this context) and the other cane cutters, he becomes immersed in a culture which values a man by the amount of cane he can cut and which fills his life with the comradeship of those with whom he lives and works. His visits to Meggie taper off as he becomes more and more a part of this male world. He repeatedly postpones leaving the cane fields, always saying they need a particular amount of additional money, but it is clear to Meggie and to the reader that there will never be enough money, that the money is just a pretext. Despite his protestations, he does not really want to leave the backbreaking work because it offers him rewards in male companionship that he does not find with a woman.

The third male society is Ralph's, the Roman Catholic hierarchy which no woman can enter since no woman can be ordained to the priesthood (though the novel does not raise this issue) and which no woman can connect with because priests are vowed to celibacy. The conflict within Ralph between man and priest, of course, is based on that requirement of celibacy, and the novel would not work if the characters were not Roman Catholic. Perhaps as a result of the absence of women (except in tangential ways—as nuns, as housekeepers), the priests create for themselves a society no less male than that of Luke in the cane fields. The scenes among priests, particularly the friendship between Ralph and his mentor, Cardinal Vittorio Scarbanza di Contini-Verchese, illustrate the intimacy which grows up between these men who are denied intimacy with women. The priests at least regret that part of their humanity must be repressed, and their sensitivity contrasts sharply with the vulgarity of the cane cutters. But their society is no less exclusive, and its exclusion of women is no less indicative of a low status for women.

McCullough does not write as a professed feminist, and in some ways her fiction, including *The Thorn Birds,* can be considered antifeminist since it makes use of patriarchal assumptions without necessarily questioning them. And yet her novel demonstrates the cruel effects of women's exclusion from men's worlds and of the harm done by relegating women to subordinate roles and to suffering.

5

An Indecent Obsession
(1981)

Published in 1981, four years after McCullough's great success with *The Thorn Birds*, her new novel's title might have seemed to promise a racy novel of sexual titillation, a description which could certainly have pertained to the content of *The Thorn Birds*. *An Indecent Obsession* does indeed have sexual content and does turn on sexual matters, but the title really refers to duty as an obsession of such strength as to make it seem indecent.

In type, *An Indecent Obsession* is a psychological novel which follows principles of dramatic construction and shows some elements of the mystery in its plotting. The psychological novel is just what its name implies, a novel which relies heavily on analysis of the psychology, what might be called the internal characterization, of the individuals in the story. Particular attention is paid to motivations, to feelings, to thoughts, and to the ways all these things affect the action or plot. In *An Indecent Obsession*, psychological pathology, or abnormality, is studied, and a number of characters are revealed. Dramatic structure as seen here entails the use of a balanced rising action, climax, and falling action. The mystery element appears principally in the later portions of the novel, in several rapid twists of the plot. As Joanne Greenberg pointed out in a perceptive review, *An Indecent Obsession* is "an old-fashioned novel, with its focus on the conflict between duty and love, a rare concern in contemporary fiction" (14). What first seems clearly to be a suicide is unexpectedly revealed to have been murder. This sort of plot reversal is typical of the mystery form, in which several possible solutions may be presented in turn, all plausibly described, before the correct solution is revealed. Because of this structure, it will be most helpful to examine first the setting and mechanics of the plot structure, which control everything that follows, then characterization as the characters are established in the early portions of the novel, followed by the climax and falling action as they are informed by both plot and characterization, and finally the themes revealed through plot and characters. The setting helps to form the basic plot, on which characterization depends. An understanding of the characters, in turn, is necessary in order to comprehend the workings of the latter parts of the novel.

SETTING

Setting in fiction refers primarily to the place or places in which a story is located, but the time of the action can also be an important aspect of setting. In the case of *An Indecent Obsession,* both place and time are important. Time is specified more precisely and is more important than geographical location. The action occurs just after hostilities have ceased at the end of World War II (in August 1945) at an Australian military hospital camp on an island in the South Pacific. The camp, which consists of several wards, each in a separate building, is temporary and soon to be evacuated. It would seem no one has ever paid much attention paid to it, and it is neglected even more now that few casualties are arriving and staff and patients expect to be sent home soon.

The unadorned buildings lack any amenities. The staff seems not particularly competent. The actual site of most of the action is the mental, or "troppo," ward, which has received its nickname because these men and the staff blame the mental conditions afflicting them on the horrors of fighting in the tropics. The important structures are the ward building with its kitchen, the nurse's office, and a nearby bathhouse. Several other buildings—a nurses' lounge and an officer's office—are used for brief and relatively unimportant scenes. The concentration on just a few interior locales gives the narrative a closed-in feeling, quite appropriate to the patients, who are themselves shut up in a kind of combined hospital-camp with little to do except wait for their release.

Some potential relief is given by a nearby beach, where patients and staff are allowed to swim, at segregated times of course. The beach which represents nature, is at first a place of escape. One of the two sexual encounters in the novel takes place on the beach. Ironically, however, this encounter is a singularly unpleasant, one, exploitative strongly unlike the one which occurs indoors and which is both passionate and tender. The beach belies its promise, and nature offers little comfort to the nurses and patients. This pattern of nature as hostile appears in other ways. The seasonal changes in the tropical climate are also generally oppressive, not refreshing. For the world of this novel, nature gives little spiritual comfort.

The timing of the novel is particularly important. Since the patients and staff know they will be going home soon, there is a pervading sense of transience. Nothing is permanent about their present life. They should be looking forward to going home, but the patients and their nurse are mostly uncertain about their futures, and even the two with the best prospects eventually must change their plans. Everything is in flux.

PLOT DEVELOPMENT

An Indecent Obsession opens with the arrival of a new patient at Sister Honour Langtry's military mental ward just at the end of World War II. Michael Wilson's addition to her small group of patients quickly upsets the equilibrium she and the already present five have established, and it is in the very complex and shocking results of that shift in balance that the plot of the novel is found. The book is carefully structured, first to entangle the psychological threads which lead to disaster and then to disentangle them dramatically with several surprising but believable plot twists.

Shakespearean drama, particularly Shakespearean tragedy, gives us useful terms for defining the structural elements of this novel. The introduction and rising action are those parts of the story which set things into motion, introduce characters and settings, establish relationships and problems of the characters, and initiate whatever conflicts will be present. The climax, which may also be referred to as the turning point, occurs when the conflict comes to its highest point and causes the action to take a different direction than had previously seemed likely. This moment of greatest emotional intensity leads to the falling action, in which the various threads of action are unraveled, often with tragic results. Although Shakespearean tragedies are structured in five acts, Mc-

Cullough's novel, which follows this conventional pattern reasonably closely, consists of seven sections.

Each of the seven sections of the novel serves a clear function or purpose in the development of its characters and themes. Part 1 introduces all the major characters and shows the beginning of the change in relationships within the ward as it begins to integrate Michael Wilson, a new patient. Part 2, complicating the situation by revealing the presence of an apparent antagonist, depicts the deep anger and nastiness of Luce Daggett and dramatizes his acting out of his anger as he seduces a nurse and has rough sex with her on the beach. The third and fourth sections are the most action filled: Part 3 psychologically and Part 4 physically. Part 3 complicates the relationships of Michael and Luce and of Michael and Sister Langtry and shows Neil, previously her confidant and friend, becoming jealous of Michael. In addition, Sister Langtry warns the young nurse who has become Luce's sexual plaything and the object of his vengeance that he is dangerous. Part 4 brings the action to a climax. Luce, enraged that Sister Langtry has warned the young nurse, threatens her, tells the other patients that Michael is homosexual (incorrect information surreptitiously read on Michael's medical records), and creates two scenes, one with a deeply disturbed patient and another in which he taunts Michael with his alleged homosexuality. Having broken up the latter confrontation, Sister Langtry takes Michael, for his protection, to her quarters, where their sexual attraction leads unexpectedly to a passionate sexual union. The remaining three sections carry to inescapable conclusions the results of the actions in the fourth section. Like the falling action after the climax of Shakespearean drama, they gradually work out the implications of these actions. In Part 5, Luce is found dead and an inquiry reinforces the initial indications that he has killed himself. Part 6 covers the evacuation of the camp and makes the surprising revelation that Luce had actually been killed by another of the patients. Finally, Part 7, a kind of afterword bringing the various plot lines to their conclusions, follows Nurse Langtry, now referred to as Honour, as she returns home, where she enrolls in additional training so she can become a nurse to the mentally ill, and reveals what has become of several of the other characters.

This structure creates a dramatic framework for the plot. The rising action, or complication, in which the various motivations and threads of action are established, stretches through the first three sections, with the first two being primarily exposition (the establishment of information the reader will need). The climax, or crisis, occurs in the fourth section, with the falling action occupying the fifth and sixth sections. The last section, then, serves as a conclusion, suggesting some meanings for the events of the novel, tidying up loose ends by explaining what has happened to some of the characters, and bringing closure (a sense of finality).

CHARACTER DEVELOPMENT

Complicated characters with shifting relationships are at the heart of this novel. Sister Honour Langtry is the central character, although her part in the action of the novel is little greater, in some senses is even less, than the parts of Luce Daggett, Michael Wilson, and perhaps even Neil Parkinson. The novel is told in a third-person point of view (that is, all characters are referred to as "he" or "she," in the third person as grammatically defined, by an outside narrative voice), with the thoughts of all the major and some of the minor characters being revealed from time to time. Sister Langtry's perspective opens and closes the novel, indicating her particular importance. Her position as protagonist, or central character, of the novel is underscored in several other ways. Her relationships with her patients are central to the action, and she is unusual in the novel in seeming to learn and grow from her experiences. Alone among the important characters, she is referred to by her title and last name. The others are always called by first names, even nicknames. Significantly, in the conclusion of the novel, when she is the only one remaining to be affected by what has happened, she is referred to by her given name.

Of the major characters, she is the only nonpatient and thus the only one for whom a psychological record is not summarized, at least briefly. For each of her patients, there has been some imputation of mental illness, even if that determination is clearly wrong. She, however, is eminently sane and, in fact, must be particularly strong and stable since a number of unstable men totally depend on her. A fully qualified nurse (the title "Sister" is given to nurses trained in the British tradition, which of course includes Australia), she had volunteered to serve in the military at the beginning of World War II, and she had served with distinction. Her posting to a mental ward was something of a demotion, but she discovered that it required all her wits and sensitivity. By the time the novel opens, she is skilled, tender, and wise in her care of her five charges.

For each of the major characters, McCullough gives extensive background information. For the patients, this comes partly in the form of brief summaries of their medical records and the diagnoses of the conditions that brought them to the mental ward. But it also includes brief histories of their lives and outlines of their family situations and war experiences. For Sister Langtry, of course, there is no medical history, but there are a family, an education, and a military record to be summarized. Her family, alone among the families of the characters of the novel, actually appears, but only in the final pages of the novel, where they are shown to be loving and supportive though they do not always understand her devotion to her profession. Her education at a prominent girls' school in Sydney and her nursing training at a leading hospital are alluded to. A love affair, which ended badly and left her more dedicated to her work, was an influential experience. Her military service had been unimpeachable, as indicated by her becoming an MBE (Member of the British Empire). Physically attractive, she is fulfilled in her work.

McCullough depicts Sister Langtry's character by dramatizing her patients' regard for her and her loving care of them. They have become dependent on her, and they love her. They refer to her as "Sis," and they are jealous of her attention. Several scenes show her caring tenderly for a man who needs tenderness or being firm with a man who requires correction. Her sharp observation, through a window, of the new patient as the novel opens indicates her perceptiveness, and its accuracy is borne out by the events which follow. Her portrayal throughout is of a young woman of competence, dedication, humor, and intelligence.

The one complication, aside from those which are natural parts of her work, emerges from her relationship with one of her patients, Neil Parkinson. Neil is the only officer among the men she cares for, and he has recovered from the emotional breakdown that brought him to Sister Langtry's care. His diagnosis had been involutional melancholia. Like Sister Langtry, Neil comes from a prosperous family. He was partly educated in England, and his loss of his Australian accent is a sign of membership in the upper class. His father is a self-made industrialist whom he scorns, and he had broken away from his family to become an artist. Before the war, he lived and painted in Greece but had finally been forced to recognize that he had no real gift, only competence, and would never become more than a rather ordinary artist. Because of his class and education, he enlisted in the army as an officer and was given a command. Again, this time with more serious consequences, he does not succeed. After initial popularity with his men, he "made a mistake, and his men paid for it" (39). The result is an immediate and total loss of confidence, a deep sense of guilt made worse by the fact that his men forgive him, and total breakdown. McCullough, as narrator, states that "his neurosis lingered on" in his "extreme self-doubt" (41), though he appears recovered and seems only to be waiting for the war to end to take up his life again.

Similar in background, Neil and Sister Langtry have begun to create a special relationship. They talk to each other in ways neither of them talks to any other patients or staff members. An unspoken agreement exists between them that, though they cannot now carry their relationship beyond the friendship of a nurse and her patient, when they are home they will take it up again as man and woman. At the beginning of the novel, they seem to be in a kind of equilibrium, content with what their relationship now is and assured that it will develop further in better circumstances in the near future. They seem to be two competent, assured people, although McCullough has indicated that Neil's recovery is not as complete as he thinks it is, and Sister Langtry's thoughts indicate some concern on her part about the therapeutic nature for Neil of her friendship with him.

The third character, the one who upsets the balance between Sister Langtry and her charges, including Neil, is Michael Wilson, the new patient whose arrival opens the novel. Unlike Neil, he is from humble origins, describing himself as a dairy farmer. Her first impression is that he is completely normal and does not belong in the mental ward, a snap diagnosis which turns out to be ironically correct. In fact, as she summarizes his medical records to her commanding officer, they show simply that he "is suspected of unsound mind following an unsavory incident" (50). He himself always states that he is perfectly sane, although he feels "as if someone has switched off all the light inside" (15). The "unsavory incident" causing him to be sent to the mental ward was nearly killing an officer in a fight. McCullough is at great pains to motivate this act clearly and believably. Flashbacks, in Michael's memory, tell of a friendship with a young man, a tormented homosexual who was convinced his sexuality was evil but could not change it. The young man had been in love with Michael, who could not return his love, though he learned tolerance for it and felt guilty for not loving him. The young man's death relieved him of a burden and that very relief added to his guilt. Then when a commanding officer, who had earlier made an advance to Michael's friend, repeated the advance to Michael, he exploded with rage and nearly committed murder. Instead of being court-martialed, he is sent to the mental ward, an easy way to avoid nastiness.

Michael has every reason for bitterness and anger, but he controls his emotions effectively.

McCullough uses the story of Michael's ill-fated friendship with the young man in several ways. It motivates the explosion that gets him sent to Sister Langtry's ward; it foreshadows later actions; and it dramatizes his innate willingness to serve. Throughout the novel, he cares for others, in little things and in large. Immediately after arriving, he takes over some of the ward's chores, and he is usually the one who brings tea or cleans up after others. More than that, however, he is sensitive to the feelings of others. He soon sees what the other patients require, and he is quick to give them emotional support as well as physical assistance. Just as he had taken his young friend under his protection, so he works with the three patients who truly need help, and to each he gives what that one most needs.

Having no homosexual inclinations of his own, he has twice been affected deeply by being approached by such advances. And the accusation of homosexuality follows him to the hospital camp, for it is in his medical records, which are secretly read by another patient. In this company of misfits, he is on one level the most sane and on another, the most troubled. He is sane because he is completely aware of reality and able to relate to others by perceiving their feelings truly. He is troubled because he is haunted by guilt for things which were completely outside his control. Almost all of his actions derive from his need to help others and his hatred of the false accusations made against him. His innate need to help others is strengthened by his sense of guilt for having failed his young homosexual friend. Thus his eventual renunciation of his love for Sister Langtry, in order to care for a comrade who needs him more than she, an independent woman, ever could is totally within character.

The last of the major characters is Luce Daggett, a villain in the mold of Shakespeare's Iago and other literary representatives of pure evil. Luce is not in the ward because of a diagnosis of mental illness. His medical records state no diagnosis of any sort, and Sister Langtry explains that he is there simply because it was the easiest way for his former commanding officer, whom Luce was blackmailing, to get rid of him. And yet Luce is actually the most dangerous of them all. Sister Langtry considers him "some sort of moral imbecile, a psychopath" (65), and her observation is in keeping with his actions throughout the novel.

Luce's principal function is to instigate violent acts on the part of others, but McCullough was at pains to motivate him so that his evil, though extreme, could be to some degree understandable. He has vivid memories of the grinding poverty of his childhood and still bitterly resents those who had more—both things and opportunities—than he. His accidental meeting with Sue Pedder, a nurse from a wealthy family with whom he had gone to primary school and whom he had hated then (his mother did her mother's laundry), becomes an important complicating factor in the action. His bitterness and desire to hurt the unsuspecting nurse cause him to seduce her and treat her with barely hidden contempt, an act inspiring Sister Langtry's warning of the nurse and Luce's resolve to avenge himself on Sister Langtry. For Luce, things are always this convoluted. One anger or resentment leads to another, and he seems to achieve a sense of power only by hurting others.

Luce's habit of resentment and anger is not the recent result of his wartime experiences. It goes back much further, partly to his childhood anger. He had left home as soon as he could and gone to Sydney, where he used his natural good looks and speaking voice to become an actor. He was just beginning to achieve some success on the stage when the war began. Typically for Luce, he resented the interruption to his career, somehow noticing the impact of the war only by its effect on him personally. When the war is over, he says, he'll be too old to succeed, and so here again his response to the world is bitterness and anger.

Luce's desire is always to hurt others and to have power over them. Transparent in his machinations, he feels no compunctions and no shame when he is caught. When Sister Langtry finds him snooping in Michael's medical records, he is unembarrassed. He does not hide his malice, seeming to be quite without any moral sense. He is as cruel to the helpless among his fellow patients as he is to those like Neil and Michael who have the mental health to stand up to him. He taunts another patient, "How does it feel to be a killer of old men and little children, Ben?" (15). Clearly, McCullough has set him up as the true villain of the novel. If it were not for him and his ruthless selfishness, none of the horrible events that so badly damage the others would occur. Ironically, it is in his death, which is the destruction of the evil he perpetrates, that his greatest damage is done. As villain, he succeeds by becoming a victim.

The other patients are less fully characterized, though each is given a sharp portrait and a personal and medical history. Benedict Maynard (called Ben), Matthew Sawyer (Matt), and Nugget Jones are all in the mental ward for clearly defined medical reasons. Ben has been diagnosed as suffering with dementia praecox, and his behavior and attitudes reveal a deeply disturbed man. His madness was triggered by an incident in which his company destroyed a village, only to learn later that there had been no enemy troops in it, only innocent natives. His attitudes toward women and toward his sexuality are profoundly abnormal. He sees females as either pure or degraded. "Women" are "light and life" (149) and Sister Langtry is "the most perfect of all women" (149), but "girls are dirty" (83). He is quiet and withdrawn when awake, but his sleep is tormented. No one seems able to reach him, except perhaps Michael, who cares gently for him and who recognizes the elements of self-hatred in his sexual revulsion. Perhaps it is Michael's own repeated confrontation of homosexuality that gives him his sensitivity, but Michael suspects that buried in Ben's insanity is fear that his own sexuality is what he would consider perverted. While others of her patients are more obviously helpless, Ben is the one Sister Langtry worries most about, the one she feels has the least possibility of surviving on his own when they all return home. She sees no other alternative than a mental hospital for him, and she believes that life in such an institution will kill him. Ironically, he is the one person who most clearly perceives and comments that Luce is "evil" (179, for example).

The two remaining patients are less important characters for the development of the plot. Each of them has a particular diagnosis which blames physical symptoms on unsound mental conditions. Matt Sawyer is blind, but no organic cause has been found, and his diagnosis is hysteria. A husband and father in civilian life, he is terrified about his return to his family and to his responsibilities of caring for them. He has concealed his blindness from his wife, adding to his fear and his guilt. It seems likely, in fact, that guilt is partly responsible for the continuation of the blindness. In some ways, his is the most intractable case, for he refuses treatment, saying that if there is an organic cause, it will be untreatable and if there isn't, there is no reason to bother. He has given up, and only the shock of his being returned to his unknowing wife seems likely to bring any change.

Nugget Jones constantly complains of various pains which include abdominal ailments and migraine headaches. As with Matt, no organic causes have been found. His diagnosis is hypochondria, and like many hypochondriacs he reads up on his various symptoms and regularly diagnoses himself. Ironically, his illness, fancied or real, is motivating him to achieve something of a medical education. Despite his constant complaining and whining about his various aches and pains, he is unusual in actually profiting in some way from his stay in Sister Langtry's ward.

Sister Langtry and her patients form the necessary nucleus of characters for the action of the novel, but a few others play minor roles, and several of those are strikingly though briefly individualized. Two of Sister Langtry's superiors, both satirically portrayed, are sharply characterized as incompetent and self-concerned functionaries. Matron, who is in charge of the nurses, cares only that no one is insubordinate to her and that when she inspects the wards the mosquito nets are tied up in a particularly intricate knot. She has no role in the action of the novel and seems to be present only because such an officer actually would exist. Her presence gives McCullough the opportunity to depict yet one more person who misunderstands or does not care about the men in Sister Langtry's ward.

Sister Langtry's medical commanding officer, however, does have a role to play in the novel's action, and he is a worthy parallel to Matron. Called "Colonel Chinstrap" behind his back because of his appearance, he is a neurologist of socially prominent and wealthy peacetime background who, like Neil, has been partly educated in the United Kingdom and has lost his Australian accent. Primarily portrayed by what he says and does, he has no interest in the patients of the mental ward and seems only to be marking time until he can return to his lucrative Sydney practice. He is both resentful and somewhat afraid of Sister Langtry's competence and interest in their mutual patients. She irritates him by demanding his attention be given to them and by being more perceptive about their needs and mental and emotional conditions than he is. His flaws become important to the novel when, near the climax, he gives a bottle of whisky to Neil, the one officer and thus the one man of his social class and the only one he sees as in any way his equal. This is, of course, quite against all rules, and when Neil shares the liquor with the others, their drunkenness is instrumental in leading to Luce's bloody death. After she discovers all this, Sister Langtry is able to use it to persuade him to maintain silence about those events.

The last character of any significance is a young nurse, Sister Sue Pedder. Shallow, selfish, and susceptible to flattery, she is easy prey to Luce. In fact, it is their meeting which instigates the dramatic action of the novel. Luce surely would have found other reasons to resent Sister Langtry and other pretexts for attempting to destroy her and his fellow patients, but she serves as a handy tool. The presence of an attractive young woman from Luce's hometown, whom he had hated and envied as a child and now sees an opportunity to take vengeance on, motivates him to typically malicious action. The name by which he calls her, "Miss Woop-Woop," from his contemptuous name for their mutual hometown, indicates his scorn of her. She is not a person to him, just a thing he uses to hurt others. That he had objective reasons to dislike what she represents is merely an added delight, but she perceives none of this. She is flattered by his attention and has no idea that anything other than true sexual attraction underlies his behavior. Her youthful thoughtlessness leads her, quite against all rules, to meet him on the beach at night, though she is perfectly aware of what his intentions are and, in fact, has tacitly agreed to them. Thus her inexperience and superficiality make her a perfect potential victim for Luce's evil. A weak character, she rationalizes some of the first indications that their sexual encounter is not motivated on his part by tenderness for her. And then she romanticizes the act when it is over, although he has used her cruelly. She refuses to recognize the brutality that underlay his surface politeness. When Sister Langtry later warns her about how dangerous Luce is, she is angry, even though she does at least suspect that Luce has no real interest in her.

As a nurse, Sister Pedder represents an opposite extreme from Sister Langtry. Where Sister Langtry is competent, cares about her patients, and has become a military nurse out of a sense of duty, Sister Pedder is not a particularly dedicated nurse, cares much more about her personal life than about her patients, and seems out of place on a military ward. Matron represents yet another extreme, the nurse who has risen to the top of her profession through scrupulous obedience to rules and who cares more about the appearance of her wards than about the condition of her patients. This small portion of a military installation contains a remarkable variety of characters, becoming almost a microcosm (or little world which represents the variety present in the great world outside it).

THE CLIMAX AND FALLING ACTION

Once the characters have been introduced and their relationships have become complicated in the novel's opening sections, the story moves inexorably to a shocking climax. That high point of action, quickly led up to in the fourth section and revealed in the fifth section, draws together all the plot strands established earlier. This highly dramatic scene of necessity changes everything for the characters concerned. Thus it is turning point as well as climax.

Most important about the situation at the crucial moment are that Sister Langtry is in love with Michael, that Luce is angry with Sister Langtry for having warned Sister Pedder about him, and that Colonel Chinstrap has given whisky to the men. The action speeds forward. Nugget has a migraine and is thus removed from participation. Luce threatens Sister Langtry, telling her that he will destroy something very precious to her. He then tells Ben that Michael is "a queen" (homosexual) and baits Ben for having killed innocent people. Matt, hearing but helpless because of his blindness, tries to comfort Ben. Neil, the officer to whom Colonel Chinstrap had spoken as an equal about the coming evacuation and had given a celebratory bottle of whisky, gets drunk with Matt and Ben. Upon discovering her hungover patients, Sister Langtry begins to clean up after them, and she walks in on an incredible scene in the bathhouse. Michael and Luce, both naked, are circling each other in fighting stance, and Luce is obscenely taunting Michael with being homosexual. Sister Langtry breaks it up, makes the others return to their barracks where she settles them down, and takes Michael to her quarters for his own protection. Unexpectedly to both of them, Michael and Sister Langtry turn to each other, and a tender sexual encounter, one in marked contrast with that between Luce and Sister Pedder, follows. At this dramatic and emotional moment, Part 4 ends.

The euphoria which opens the fifth section, as Sister Langtry dreams of her future with Michael, is quickly ended by her discovery of Luce's body in the bathhouse. This most violent act of the novel occurs offstage, as it must in order for the reader to be misled about the way in which Luce has died. Sister Langtry immediately realizes that Luce's brutal death—he had been slashed and his sexual organs mutilated—destroys any chance that she and Michael might have had for happiness together. Plot and character combine here as she recognizes that their joint, if differing, responsibility for Luce's apparent suicide will separate them. And her anger is at Luce—that he has won, that he has (as he had threatened) destroyed something very precious to her.

At this point, the action requires several sorts of cleaning up: the physical cleansing of the bathhouse, the protection of Sister Langtry's patients from any emotional damage caused by these events, and the silencing of potential gossip about Luce's suicide and its causes. The immediate aftermath is easily taken care of, and a cover-up is soon under way. Luce's death is officially pronounced a suicide, and medical explanations for how he could have managed to inflict those particular wounds upon himself are contrived. Sister Langtry tries to ensure that there are no lasting effects of the ugliness on any of her patients and that neither the drunkenness of several of the patients before and presumably during the suicide nor the sexual liaison of herself and Michael during its occurrence will be revealed. She commits a kind of moral blackmail in order to achieve these results when she lets Colonel Chinstrap know she is aware of his infraction in supplying Neil with liquor.

McCullough has carefully placed her major characters so that they lack particular pieces of the puzzle. Michael and Sister Langtry know nothing of Luce's death, and Neil and the others know nothing of Michael's and Sister Langtry's liaison. Readers know of the liaison but are kept ignorant until later of what went on among the men after Sister Langtry took Michael to her quarters. As through much of the novel, Sister Langtry's is the most often used point of view, which restricts the information presented and enables McCullough to create suspense through the reader's lack of knowledge. After the official verdict of suicide is established, the ward is left in a state of uncertainty. Various characters misunderstand each other, with the mutual misperceptions of Michael and Sister Langtry being particularly poignant. Guilt and pain torment most of them, to the point that their community is destroyed. The coming evacuation once partly feared precisely because it would break up that community, now seems a longed-for escape.

Nevertheless, some elements of the old community still remain. It is gradually revealed that the men have made several agreements among themselves and that there is a second cover-up beneath the obvious cover-ups surrounding the events of the night Luce died. The mutual concern of the men for each other persists, even though it may now be motivated as much by guilt as by affection. They have agreed—have made a "pact" (250). One of its implications seems to be that Neil will take care of Matt, and by extension his family, when they all return to Australia. In parallel fashion, Michael will care for Ben. Thus the two most helpless of the men, the blind and the clearly insane, will be protected.

But the pact also includes the banding together of the five remaining men to keep something from Sister Langtry. The imbalancing of her relationship with them, which occurred the night of Luce's death, removed her from her position as their protector and confidante. She has become both an outsider and someone they feel they must protect. Only Michael, who was not present because he was with her when those events occurred, argues against secrecy, and finally, because he thinks he owes her an explanation of his withdrawal from her, he tells her the truth. Luce did not kill himself. Ben's sexual mania and his belief that Luce had destroyed Michael resulted in Ben's killing Luce. The mutilation of Luce's genitals is explained by Ben's warped sexuality, not by some hypothetical sexual revulsion of Luce's, which would in any case have been completely out of character. Michael is overcome by guilt. He considers his staying with Sister Langtry to have been weakness and betrayal. If he had returned to the others, Ben would have known he was safe and would not have killed Luce. It is finally his overwhelming sense of responsibility, in keeping with his behavior from the time he took his young homosexual friend under his protection, which forces him to renounce any chance of happiness with Sister Langtry and to devote himself to Ben's care.

One last confrontation occurs before the evacuation is complete, this one between Neil and Sister Langtry. Neil explains the cover-up of Ben's murder of Luce from the point of view of those who, unlike Michael, had actually been in a position to prevent the killing. He accuses her of indirect complicity because of her shift of attention to Michael and away from the rest of them, which set up conditions leading to the murder. She accuses him of manipulating the situation so that she and Michael will renounce each other, and she realizes that if she betrayed them by turning to Michael, they had betrayed her by concealing the murder. There seems plenty of guilt to go around, and there is no more chance for Neil and Sister Langtry than there is for Michael and Sister Langtry. The only relationships remaining from this tragedy are two very unequal ones of caretaker and patient: Neil and Matt, and Michael and Ben.

One more section, Part 7, remains to bring closure. It centers around Sister Langtry, now referred to as Honour, an appropriate name for she does act throughout with honor. First she discusses her experiences and goals with her mother, and then she enters training as a nurse for the mentally ill, a step backward professionally but one she has become deeply committed to as a result of her experiences as a nurse to the "troppos" she had cared for in the final days of the war. She learns that Matt has died; his blindness actually had an undetected organic cause. Thus Neil has been freed of part of his burden. Tragically, she also learns, Michael had failed in his attempt to protect Ben and keep him from being institutionalized. Ben had tried to kill a man who was attacking Michael. Unlike Luce's death, this violent outbreak could not be covered up, and Michael had killed Ben and then himself. Ben is saved from being imprisoned or institutionalized, but at a supreme cost. The novel ends with Honour's realization that now she could reestablish her relationship with Neil, but she makes a final renunciation. Her nursing is more important to her, more a duty than any love for a man who does not need her as much as her patients.

The impact of the events at the center of this psychological study is both tragic and hopeful. Lives are destroyed because of malice and failed responsibility and guilt, but Honour at least reestablishes the central purpose of her life, nursing, with a new direction, the care of the mentally incapacitated. The rapid movement from climax through the falling action brings a final resolution which is tragic for most of the other characters.

THEMATIC ISSUES

Themes, the abstract ideas illustrated by or discussed in a work of fiction, may be present in various levels of such a work. In *An Indecent Obsession*, an obvious theme illustrated on the level of plot is homosexuality. It is presented as something abnormal, perverse, to be recoiled from or at least hidden. Some readers may consider aspects of the use of this theme to be homophobic, but this would be missing the point. Homosexuality is used as a plot device to motivate Michael's behavior, to give Luce a way to harm Michael, and to explain Ben's insane violence.

What is really illustrated by the novel are the social effects of homophobia, or hatred of homosexuality. The date at which the action takes place is significant here. In 1945 homosexuality was everywhere considered a perversion. The social stigma was much greater and more universal then than it is in the 1990s. Homosexuality—or fear of homosexuality—was a useful device for this novel, enabling McCullough to frame relationships or potential relationships which would entail shame or guilt, themes more important to the novel. Homosexuality itself is not present in the novel, only referred to in a flashback to the dead young friend of Michael's who was tormented because he believed homosexuality was evil and because he could not eradicate it from his feelings.

Though homosexual acts do not occur, homosexuality as a theme has relevance to a number of characters. Ben, insecure in his sense of self, has fears about his sexuality. Luce, truly perverse in many ways, is perfectly willing to use his sexuality to manipulate others, in either homosexual or heterosexual relationships. Indeed, as a young man beginning to make his way in Sydney, he had prostituted himself with both men and women, caring only what he could get from them. For him, there is no shame. He will use sexuality in any way he can in order to manipulate others. Homosexuality is just a handy accusation he can make to harm those he wishes to damage.

Michael is accused, wrongly, of being homosexual. When he twice, before the novel opens, received homosexual advances, he rejected them, once with pity and regret and once with rage. The rage was not for the fact of the homosexuality but rather from the fear that an old burden of responsibility was beginning again. His strength is seen in the fact that, despite the great harm done him by his experiences, he is tolerant. "I reckon homosexuals are like any other group of men, some good, some bad, and some indifferent" (241), he says when he is being questioned in the investigation into Luce's death, at a time when he might be most resentful. This evenhandedness helps to indicate that it is not homosexuality which is a target of attack in the novel but homophobia, which is being revealed as a dangerous attitude that can lead to misunderstandings, even to violence.

More meaningful in the novel, because they are used as themes acted out by the characters, not simply devices to motivate and move the plot, are two pairs of abstract qualities: shame and guilt, on one hand; and love and duty, on the other. Connecting these related themes is the question of identity or self. Shame and (in part) guilt are related to the theme of homosexuality. Shame may be distinguished from guilt by the presence of a social component. One feels shame for acts one knows to be held in contempt by society, and the shame refers to the scorn one expects from others. Guilt, on the other hand, refers to acts one considers morally wrong on some absolute scale, whether or not anyone else knows about them. The theme of shame is introduced in connection with Michael's young friend, who is full of shame for his homosexual feelings, which he believes to be evil. He strives to control them and hates himself because he cannot. Luce, who is himself shameless, tries to play on the shame he expects Michael to feel for his alleged homosexuality.

The theme of guilt also relates to the homosexual theme but less directly. Michael feels guilt because he cannot love his young homosexual friend as the friend wishes. However, this theme also pertains to almost all of the major characters in varying degrees and in varying ways. Ben is filled with guilt for the incident in which his company destroyed an innocent village. Neil struggles with guilt over the mistake which cost the lives of some of his men. However, this theme is most fully developed after the climax of Luce's death. Most obviously, Michael and Sister Langtry are separated by their respective guilt for this bloody event. After Sister Langtry learns the truth about Ben's murder of Luce and the men's subsequent cover-up, her thoughts summarize the collective nature of their guilt. "Knowing what they had done had freed her from a large measure of the guilt she might otherwise have preserved over her conduct toward them. If they thought she had betrayed them in turning to Michael, she knew they had betrayed her. For the rest of their lives they would have to live with Luce Daggett. So would she" (294). This kind of guilt is less tangible than the direct responsibility for Luce's death which belongs to Ben, but it is no less powerful in its effects on the individuals feeling it. McCullough has developed this theme most significantly by dramatic means, demonstrating instead of telling.

Feelings of shame and guilt are connected to the senses of self felt by many of the characters. Some of them lack a secure sense of who they are. Luce's profession of actor, one who continually plays roles, symbolizes his own lack of any real center, his lack of a true self Michael knows who he is but finds his selfhood repeatedly under attack when he is accused of homosexuality. Sister Langtry generalizes of her patients, who seem preoccupied with themselves, that their "apparent self-orientation . . . was only evidence of lack of self" (29). She strives to keep her own sense of self out of her relationships with her patients, believing that proper professionalism requires objectivity which can be achieved only by reining in her own feelings. Repeatedly, comments are made which reflect on a hollowness of individual patients, a failure to have secure self-knowledge. They have all been changed by the war, and these changes have impinged on their senses of identity. In some cases, those changes are what have brought them to the mental ward.

The climax and resolution of the novel clarify and reemphasize the selfhood of the characters, bringing little new change. Nugget is an exception. He seems ready to prepare for some sort of medical work, a result of the reading his hypochondria has inspired. But for most, recognition and understanding, rather than change, tend to be the result. Neil's return to the family with which he had broken is not really an exception, for his awareness of his lack of potential as an artist had predated his war experiences. Luce is destroyed because of his malice, because of the emptiness inside that made him strive to harm others. Michael continues to bear his burden of caring for the weak. For Ben and Matt, so badly damaged, there is no potential for new understanding. Matt dies of a brain tumor, and Ben has one more violent episode, leading to his own death and that of Michael. Sister Langtry alone, except for Nugget, takes a new path, when she retrains to become a nurse for mental patients, but this is really a rededication to her primary profession. It is simply a change in specialty caused by her experience during the war. After a brief period of believing she might find fulfillment in love and marriage, she returns to her first definition of herself, as a nurse before she is a woman.

Basic to all these themes, as indicated by the meaning of the novel's title, are the twin themes of love and duty. They refer most prominently to Sister Langtry, one compelling reason for considering her the protagonist. Early in the novel, she is depicted mainly in connection to her duty as nurse, a job she loves and performs well. Her only nonprofessional behavior in the book's early pages is found in her friendship with Neil. However, as the story complicates itself and she becomes more and more attracted to Michael, she begins to see love and duty as separate from each other and in conflict. She feels she will have to choose. What the other men see as her rejection of them in favor of Michael may be interpreted as her choosing love and spurning duty. Here the theme of guilt combines with the themes of love and duty, for it is that choice of love that is partly instrumental in Luce's death and for which she feels guilt. Only in the novel's last pages, when Michael is gone and she briefly considers reestablishing contact with Neil, does she determine finally that love and duty are for her the same, that her patients need her and she needs them and loves to serve them. The last line of the novel clarifies her final "understanding that duty, the most indecent of all obsessions, was only another name for love" (324). Thus McCullough finally sums up the central meanings of the novel in this rededication of Sister Langtry to her work.

A FEMINIST READING OF *AN INDECENT OBSESSION*

As pointed out in the feminist reading of *The Thorn Birds*, feminist criticism rests on certain social, psychological, and economic assumptions. Principal among these are the beliefs that women are as important as men, that they have all the same innate abilities and needs as men, and that they should be treated equally with men and given all the same opportunities. This implies that they should receive equal pay for equal or equivalent work and not be segregated in a few acceptable occupations, such as teaching, nursing, and secretarial work. Allied with those assumptions is the observation that women rarely are treated equally and that they labor at severe disadvantages in today's world. Feminist criticism, as it is currently practiced, is one of many outgrowths of the contemporary feminist movement, which began in the 1960s. One of the approaches feminist critics take is the examination of the themes and characters of fiction, in order to show whether and how fictional works support or deny feminist assumptions and observations. With Mc-Cullough, by no means a feminist writer although one who has created a gallery of interesting female characters, one task of the feminist critic is to examine the clash of her somewhat overtly anti- (or at least non-) feminist ideas and attitudes with her creation of strong female characters who live in rather feminist ways.

An Indecent Obsession is by no means a feminist novel. Women, with the exception of Sister Langtry, are generally portrayed negatively. Sister Pedder, a happy and shallow sex-object, and Matron, the caricature of a masculinized woman in power, represent a very negative view of professional women. And even Sister Langtry and her friend and confidante, Sister Dawkin (apparently the only other competent medical person at the hospital camp), do not have a favorable idea of women. As these two nurses are thinking about their coming return to civilian nursing, Sister Dawkin grumbles about the demands made by women patients, with Sister Langtry's tacit agreement. There seems little female solidarity here, although the warm friendship between the two nurses serves as a nice example of female bonding.

Sister Langtry's ideas of what it is to be female seem quite stereotypical. When she is caught in the struggle between love and duty, she thinks that "the void between reason and her own feminine feelings was unbridgeable" (231). She accepts the conventional notion that men have reason and women have feelings and that women's feelings are irrational. Later, when she and Michael meet for the last time, she defines what love means to her: "It means sharing my life with you! . . . Living with you! Keeping your home, having your babies, growing old together" (279). This surprisingly domestic definition suggests her willingness to subordinate herself to Michael and to give up the profession which had been her primary way of defining herself. Even more strikingly, when Michael points out that all her "apprenticeship" had been toward nursing, not toward domesticity, and suggests that love as she defines it is not what he needs, she pleads with him that she desperately needs his love, that she cannot be fulfilled without it. The conventional notion that a woman can be fulfilled only through being a wife and mother, while a man finds fulfillment in his work, seems to underlie her uncharacteristic outburst here. In an ironic twist, it is actually Michael who needs to be needed and to care for someone else and Sister Langtry who needs to be guided by a professional duty. Understanding their differing needs better than she does, he points out that almost any woman can do what she says she wants but that few can do what she actually does. Neither of them realizes that what he is describing is a reversal of the usual gender roles while what she says she wants is quite in line with societal expectations. She must return, as she does at the end of the novel, to her original focus on nursing, in order to find fulfillment.

It is glaringly ironic that Sister Langtry lives a more feminist life and makes more feminist decisions than she is aware. Like others of McCullough's female characters, she is strong and wise, and it is through her strength and wisdom that she makes her life and finds contentment. It should be noted, though, that the work which is at the center of her sense of self and duty is in one of the most stereotypically female professions, one based on caring for and serving others. *An Indecent Obsession* illustrates a feminist lifestyle and supports some feminist ideas even while it undercuts basic feminist assumptions and goals.

The last portion of the novel contains several examples of bird imagery. Just after her final break with Michael, Sister Langtry sees two terns flying together against a beautiful sky and likens their beauty and freedom to what she had wanted with Michael (282). On the novel's last page, as she realizes that there is nothing for her with Neil, she remembers Michael and his wisdom that knew a "strong bird needs room to fly" (324). She is that bird and must fly alone, but she had to be taught this lesson by a man.

6

A Creed for the Third Millennium
(1985)

Readers accustomed to McCullough's realistic novels of the present and recent past with their Australian and South Pacific settings must have been surprised at the new departure of her fourth novel. *A Creed for the Third Millennium* (1985) resembles its predecessors principally in its length and its complexity. It differs in setting, types of characters, thematic meanings, plot—in fact, in just about every important respect. This new book is again a novel of ideas, even more obviously than *An Indecent Obsession.* It uses the United States, a new setting for her, as its location. But this is a United States of the future, in which she predicts the effects of certain trends observed in the present. Thus instead of making her story and characters her primary concerns, as in most of her earlier fiction, McCullough here is most interested in the social, political, and ecological conditions which surround her plot and motivate her characters. She has called it "my pessimistic novel of the future" (Steinberg 110). The reception of this new book was unenthusiastic. One reviewer lambasted it, saying it "could well be the most perfectly awful novel ever published" (Gray 80). Another found parts of it "embarrassing" but also declared that there is "a treasure in the middle comprised of some of the spiritual messages put into the mouth of [its protagonist]" (Mitchell 6).

It is an old literary device to set a story in a future in order to evaluate something in the present or to argue for some particular action in the present. Stories which depict good future societies, ones which have managed to solve problems of the author's present and thus suggest solutions to those problems, are called "utopias," a name coming from an early outstanding example of the genre, Sir Thomas More's *Utopia*, published in 1516. More called his ideal society "Utopia" from Greek words meaning "no place" and "good place." In the increasing pessimism of the twentieth century, many writers have chosen to use a technique which is essentially the opposite of More's. These writers, who depict troubled, oppressive societies, create what are called "dystopias," a word meaning "bad places." Among the best-known novels in this tradition are George Orwell's *1984* (1949) and Aldous Huxley's *Brave New World* (1932). The crucial elements of a dystopia are that it show a hostile world and that the causes of its problems be clearly related to conditions in the author's own time and place. The author, then, predicts what will be the effects of phenomena he or she sees as potentially dangerous. This is the tradition of *A Creed for the Third Millennium*.

SETTING

For this dystopian novel, McCullough chose an American setting some forty-five years in her future. Extrapolating (that is, predicting what will occur in the future by drawing possible conclusions from selected aspects of a present situation) from current political and social trends, she imagines what the United States might come to be. She chooses the early years of the twenty-first century, always referred to as the "third millennium," or simply the "millennium," the beginning of the third period of a thousand years in our calendar. The use of the term reminds historically minded readers of the fears that greeted the beginning of the second millennium, the year 1000, when many people believed that the Second Coming of Christ, and thus the end of the world, was at hand. Much social unrest was the result. At the beginning of McCullough's new millennium, the international political structure has changed from what was known in the 1980s when the novel was written. Throughout the book, occasional reminders of political changes occur. For instance, a Eurocommune and an Arabicommune share power with the United States, and England no longer recognizes a king, apparently because of its Communist government, though that sovereign is still recognized as the King of Australia and New Zealand (376).

A mini ice age has begun. Mitchell points out that this is never explained, though it contradicts current theories about global warming (6). Normal temperatures have declined, and the effect on daily life and on the economic structure of the United States is enormous. Winters are colder, summers shorter and cooler. The landmass available for people to live on is shrinking, while population in the developed world had continued to grow in the latter portions of the twentieth century. Large parts of the United States are no longer comfortably inhabitable year round. The population has shifted southward, partly voluntarily and partly as a result of government relocation projects. Such relocation is partly permanent and partly seasonal. Atlanta is replacing New York as the cultural and economic center of the United States. Northern cities have become ghost towns in winter, and the trend is toward their complete desertion.

The impact of the ice age is as strong in family and personal life as it is in the political life of the nation. At some time in the past—no date is given—a fictitious Delhi Treaty has restricted family size in the developed world, following the example of actual Chinese policy. Most couples in the United States are allowed to have only one child. However, a few are permitted a second child, and the selections by the Second Child Bureau of the fortunate families have extremely divisive results. Those applicants who are refused are understandably resentful and angry, causing much social unrest, especially when it appears that favoritism has affected the lottery which officially makes the selections. The goal is "World Human Population Energy Equilibrium, always referred to as WHOOPEE" (18). As is suggested by this use of a rather silly acronym (making the initials of an agency or, as here, a function, into a word), the government is excessively bureaucratic.

The places in which the action principally occurs are the fictional city of Holloman, Connecticut, and Washington, D.C. In addition, brief scenes in later portions of the novel are set in a variety of cities throughout the United States, with the final tragic scene occurring on an island off the eastern coast of North Carolina. Holloman (phonetically, "hollow man," a brief characterization of the people living in this world) is the home of the central character and his family, and it also serves as an example of a dying northern city. It is described as overwhelmingly "grey" (McCullough's preferred British English spelling). The inner city is largely unpopulated, and complete desertion of the city seems not far off. The central character and his family remain in Holloman out of love for what the city used to be. They run a psychological clinic and feel a sense of duty to help those remaining there battle against an inescapable depression. The primary Holloman setting consists of two large houses which have been combined. One serves as a home and the other as an office and clinic. The decor in the home is white, in order to reflect light and heat, and the windows are boarded up in order to conserve heat. But what is most striking is the presence of plants everywhere. A long paragraph lists the varieties (19), and the family's regular Sunday activity is caring for the plants—watering, pruning, washing, feeding, spraying, and so on. The plants filter and perfume the air. Though McCullough does not stress this point, they would seem to be a weapon against air pollution.

The psychological effects of the ice age and of population controls are as important as the physical results. People have been uprooted. Maternal and paternal instincts are thwarted by the stringent controls on family size. Organized religion has dwindled away, being seen as either irrelevant or a betrayal. Most important is the nearly universal depression. People tend to be nostalgic for a past that they remember but cannot return to; as a result, they feel hopeless. Treating this malady has come to be the specialty of the protagonist's psychological practice.

Contrasting with Holloman is Washington, D.C., the seat of political power. A new cabinet-level department, the Department of the Environment, is central. Action occurs in the offices of that agency, depicted as "utterly soulless" (37), and in the White House, particularly the Oval Office. The presence of the cherry blossoms in springtime, occurring much later than formerly, and the use of the Lincoln Memorial as a setting for a mass demonstration are reminders of the Washington of the 1980s when the book was written. These settings help to give readers a sense of familiarity with a country radically different from the one they know.

The depiction of government is not favorable. The presidency and a single cabinet department are shown, but the other major branches of government, Congress and the Supreme Court, are notable by their absence. The only significant mention of either of them comes in the appearance of one senator as a very minor character. Power is in the administrative branch. And that power is wielded in a cynical way. The political figures depicted are generally more concerned with their own careers than with their service to the public.

In dystopias, setting becomes of primary importance. Specific places may even act almost as characters. In *A Creed for the Third Millennium,* the time of the action is of particularly great importance, and time, combined with the nature of the society and the hostile climate, undergirds and supports the entire structure of the novel, including plot, characters, and themes.

PLOT DEVELOPMENT

Basically, *A Creed for the Third Millennium* tells the story of Dr. Joshua Christian, identified as the one man who can inspire the American people to the reawakening which will enable them to surmount the dire situation in which they find themselves. The novel follows him as he accepts his mission, becomes ever more committed to it, and finally is destroyed by what has become an obsession. The story is told in a generally straightforward chronology, though occasionally it must backtrack to narrate events which are occurring at the same time. This happens particularly in the novel's climactic scenes, when action is rapidly and simultaneously taking place both in Washington and on an island off the North Carolina coast.

In structure (that is, in organization), the narrative falls into four main sections of unequal length. First (chapters I to III) is the search, by the Department of the Environment, for a person who can inspire the people of the United States somehow to save themselves from their despair. This section concludes with the identification of Dr. Joshua Christian as that man. The second section (chapters IV to VII) covers the period in which he is assisted in the writing of the book which is to be the vehicle through which he carries out his mission. A transitional scene (chapter VIII), occurring when Joshua appears on a popular television show, opens the depiction of his actual mission, the third section (chapter IX to the middle of chapter XI). That mission, his appealing directly to and inspiring the people, is carried out through his tour publicizing the book. Again a transition scene occurs, shifting to the climax of the mission, a triumphal march from New York to Washington (the last portion of chapter XI). After the triumph comes tragedy, in the final section (chapters XII and XII, which end the book), as Joshua suffers complete physical and mental breakdown. He commits suicide, and the ending of the novel mixes indications that he has failed with hints that his message will continue to live on, even if corrupted and manipulated by some of his followers.

The basic plot, then, is relatively simple. However, the narrative is filled with incident, and it follows dramatic changes in Joshua and in his sense of his mission and of himself. It also depicts in detail the changing relationships between Joshua and the members of his family, the public, and especially Dr. Judith Carriol (the career functionary at the Department of the Environment who is responsible for his being identified as the person to undertake the mission of revitalizing the people). It might be argued, in fact, that there are two parallel plots, one following Joshua and his mission from his point of view, and the other following the attempts of the President, the Secretary of the Environment, and Dr. Carriol to use his charismatic gifts for their own purposes. Joshua wishes to serve; the others wish to cement or build their own power.

A slightly fuller analysis of the plot will show how these devices work themselves out. The novel opens by introducing Joshua, his setting in Holloman and his psychological clinic, and his large and loving family. Then it moves to Washington and deliberations within a think tank in the Department of the Environment which has undertaken a top secret "Operation Search." To everyone's surprise, the little known Joshua Christian turns out to fit all the requirements set up. After he is identified, Judith Carriol, who has initiated and directed the search, dismisses those who have worked on the project and puts "Operation Messiah," the second and even more secret phase, into operation. Among the few who are informed are the President and the Secretary of the Environment. Joshua himself is not told how he is being used. Judith simply persuades him to write a book and then marshals her power to supply a ghostwriter and a publisher (all this is underwritten by the government, unbeknownst to Joshua). Joshua is persuaded that through a book he can reach many more people than through his private practice. His motives are completely idealistic and selfless.

The first stages go well. Joshua and his ghostwriter work effectively together and his book, called *God in Cursing: A New Approach to Millennial Neurosis,* seems to be a kind of self-help book which defines and describes for a popular audience the psychological problem he has observed and treated in his private practice. The book also offers inspirational tips for overcoming that condition. It is an immediate bestseller. Joshua's appearance on a late-night television show makes him an instant public figure. The following publicity tour is an overwhelming success. Crowds follow him everywhere, and his impact on both the public as a whole and on individuals is powerful. But McCullough is careful to indicate that the seeds of Joshua's destruction are present even in his early success. He gradually becomes more and more caught up in the emotion of the crowds and more and more persuaded of his own mission. Almost accidentally he begins walking with groups of those who have come to see him, and this practice soon becomes obsessive.

First walking from place to place within cities, he graduates to walking between cities. His purpose initially is to have more time to talk with individuals, but the walking becomes an end in itself.

As the tone (or mood) changes, Judith becomes worried about his physical and mental condition and persuades first the President and then Joshua himself to bring a conclusion to the tour with one last ceremonial and triumphant walk from Washington, D.C. to New York, billed as the "March of the Millennium." By the time it begins, Joshua is physically disintegrating from the months and miles of walking without caring for himself. He is also collapsing mentally because of his obsession with his mission and with his role as a savior of the American people (and even the people of the world, for *God in Cursing* has been translated into other languages and family members have gone abroad to publicize it).

As the novel winds to its dramatic conclusion, McCullough skillfully weaves together a number of plot strands. Apparently unrelated events lead inexorably to disaster. Joshua is completely irrational. Judith arranges for him to be sent to an island hideaway where he can be secretly cared for by highly trained medical personal. But a number of accidents, most of them well motivated and prepared for, intervene. The Secretary of the Environment, who should have made the arrangements and then later met with the President to explain what had happened, is drunk and does not follow Judith's directions. His secretary, exhausted from working constantly for weeks, falls asleep and does not rouse her employer. The pilot crashes his helicopter shortly after leaving Joshua at the empty estate, and no oil slick appears to give the alarm since he had decided to delay filling the plane in order to expedite the flight. Alone on the island and totally demented, Joshua kills himself.

The last few pages recount the discovery of Joshua's body and subsequent attempts made by the government to defuse the possible effects of his death. There is concern either that angry crowds might riot or that he might be made a martyr, in either case destroying the morale built by his positive message. These last pages also reveal Judith's cementing of her own position of power. Like Joshua, the reader must wonder what has been the point of it all.

CHARACTER DEVELOPMENT

Joshua Christian and Judith Carriol are the characters who move the plot. Not surprisingly, they are also the most fully developed. Joshua, as the protagonist or central character, is at the hub of the action and themes of the novel, and he is the most complex and completely drawn, as well as the character who changes most dramatically. Judith is also a very complicated character, but instead of changing, she is revealed increasingly fully as the plot unwinds. These two very dissimilar people are brought together by the social, political, and climatic situation of the United States in the year 2032. Each has a particular mission to fulfill, and it is in the working out of their missions that McCullough characterizes them. Joshua's mission is to save the psychological and spiritual health of the people of the United States and subsequently of the world. Judith's goals are to enable Joshua to fulfill his mission and at the same time to ensure her own political career and power.

Dr. Joshua Christian is a very dynamic character. Analyzing his characterization means following the changes he undergoes. A clinical psychologist by profession, at the beginning of the novel he heads a successful clinic. Still unmarried at the age of thirty-two, he is assisted in his clinic by other members of his close-knit and supportive family. He loves his Connecticut city, despite the inconveniences and discomforts of living so far north during this ice age. However, from the very beginning, he has a sense of destiny, an almost religious sense of a calling or vocation that is unfulfilled. He has a strange feeling that there is something he must do despite vague sensations of dread. Although he is little known in his profession, he has an enthusiastic following among those who have been his patients and who consider him almost a miracle worker.

He is depicted as a brilliant and caring clinician, who is deeply concerned with his patients and with the nature of the depression that he sees among them. The strongest and most obvious elements of that depression, which he has given the name of "millennial neurosis," are related, on one hand, to the cold weather and the growing necessity to relocate to the south and, on the other, to the prohibition of repeated childbearing. His gift as a psychologist is his ability to concentrate intensely on his patients, to hear them completely. This ability is partly responsible for his charisma, a quality Judith had insisted must be present in the person identified by Operation Search and a quality which he quickly proves to have.

McCullough portrays Joshua as somewhat naive. He never realizes what his actual assignment is or that he is being subtly manipulated, and he is first surprised and then delighted to be given the opportunity to write a book. Through it, he realizes, he can reach millions of people who are suffering from millennial neurosis instead of the very few individuals he can personally treat. However, a man of relationships and not of the written word, he has a severe case of writer's block, and a ghostwriter does the actual composition of the book. *God in Cursing*, the result of his collaboration with a gifted writer, takes its title from a poem by Elizabeth Barrett Browning which reads in part, "Get leave to work . . . for God, in cursing, gives us better gifts than men in benediction" (192). The title sums up much of his philosophy, which is also his explanation of and his cure for what he calls millennial neurosis. The curse of the current difficulties, it suggests, is also a great opportunity for change and growth. That neurosis is, in his view, a result of contemporary responses to the severe climate and to population controls. He sees contemporary humanity as filled with disappointment in having lost an easy life and with a useless nostalgia for what can not be recaptured. This explains the term "millennial": all the events and occurrences that have created the culture of Joshua's world came together about the time of his birth, in the year 2000, the beginning of a new millennium or period of 1,000 years. Just as people had responded to powerful fears in the medieval world when the year 1000 approached and many people thought the Second Coming of Christ would soon occur, so now they have reacted to the changes of this new millennium with despair. His solution is for people to look to the future, to work hard, to accept what they must and go forward. He calls himself a "meliorist" (129), a person who believes things will get better, and he suggests that when the generation of people who knew a better past has died off, the new generation, which has never known an easy life, will be better able to cope with their new situation. At that point, millennial neurosis will cease to exist.

Buoyed by his sense of mission and his awareness of having a message of practical usefulness, Joshua is overjoyed when the book is published to a warm reception. His strength and enthusiasm grow. He feeds off the excitement of the crowds as his publicity tour for the book proceeds, and he begins to change. Or perhaps it is not so much a change as an intensification of what was already in him. His sense of mission increases, and he becomes increasingly more obsessed with his need to be with and to help people. He drives himself harder and harder, both physically and emotionally. Gradually, he becomes confused about exactly who he is and what his mission is. Idolized by millions of people, he begins sometimes to see himself as somehow godlike. At the same time, however, he insists that he is purely human. His message stresses that people can control their own fates, that they must take charge for

themselves. He cannot accept the premise that an outside force is exert-
ing power, even if that outside force is acting through him. As he had
first explained himself to Judith, he had stressed his belief in God—and
his conviction that the people needed to have their faith in God restored.
But his God is never well defined, has nothing to do with organized
religion, has in fact no real relevance to the current situation. Human
beings must, Joshua tells Judith, "learn to live with God *and* self at the
center of their personal universes" (100). God is transcendent, beyond
human comprehension. Thus when Joshua begins to become confused
about his own humanity, he is deeply troubled. On one hand, he begins
to see himself as Messianic; on the other, he insists that he cannot be
other than completely human. If he is somehow divine then all his work
and ultimately his suffering are meaningless lies.

The changes in him escalate as the publishing tour continues. Mc-
Cullough introduces a variety of little incidents which reveal his becoming continually more caught up in the emotion of those coming to him
for help. He pushes himself harder and harder, until finally in a dramatic
confrontation Judith accuses him of "egomania," of "being on a god
trip" (324). Her anger and harsh words make explicit what he has been
struggling with. He is tormented, insisting to himself that he must be "a
man" in order to "help Man" (326). But the people have worshipped
him, have knelt before him—and he now feels that their adoration and
his allowing of that adoration have betrayed his mission. From this moment of agony, he never recovers. His physical condition rapidly dete-
riorates, and he gradually becomes irrational.

When he leads the march from New York to Washington, he is physically almost completely incapacitated. His body is a shocking mass of
open sores and bruises. McCullough presents him as having been so
obsessed with his walking that he has forgotten about and abused his
body. He has driven himself into physical disintegration, followed rapidly by mental deterioration. By what should have been the last day of
the march, he is so weakened physically and so out of touch mentally
that he cannot continue. He has become insane, "demented," in a word
appearing often in the narrative. The charismatic man who once knew
exactly who he was and how he could help others has been transformed
into a lunatic. He continues denying his divinity, but he is so obsessed
with his likeness to Christ as the Son of God that he imitates Christ's
death. In his dementia, he seems to believe that by crucifying himself
like Christ he can prove that "a mortal man with no more god in him
than any other man" (413) can do as much as Christ could.

McCullough took on several challenges in her depiction of Joshua. First, she had to make his charisma believable and his message clear. Readers needed to be persuaded that he and his message could have the powerful personal effect on people and crowds required by the plot of the novel. Second, she had to make his change and deterioration believable. They had to have their origins in who he was at the beginning of the novel, and they had to be explained as the novel proceeded. Finally, his madness and suicide had to develop naturally and believably from what went before. The strong, happy, controlled man of the beginning must alter in such a way that readers can believe he can become the lost soul of the concluding pages. McCullough meets these challenges partly by her skillful use of foreshadowing—by introducing early the notion of a mission felt by Joshua and by showing how this sense of mission defines and redefines itself.

In characterizing Judith Carriol, McCullough's challenges were quite different. For this character, change was not required but the presence of almost contradictory qualities was. To analyze her characterization is to describe contradictions, not change. Judith must be presented as attractive and manipulative, public spirited and personally ambitious throughout the story. The challenge was to make this complicated mixture of characteristics believable. What changes as the novel moves forward is the relative emphasis on these various aspects of her personality. Judith's attractive and public-spirited side is most obvious early on, and her manipulativeness seems benign, because it is used for good purposes, through much of the earlier part of the novel. In the later stages of Joshua's deterioration, Judith's manipulativeness and ambition are most obvious and distasteful.

Judith is an important official at the Department of the Environment, in charge of a major section within the Department and the originator and developer of Operation Search. An attractive woman, she has risen from poverty by intelligence, hard work, and persistence. In her meetings with her subordinates, she shows that she is an effective and efficient leader. She also reveals her manipulativeness when she takes control of the second phase of the project without allowing those who have headed portions of the first phase even to know of the initiation of the second phase—on which they had confidently expected to work. She has all the qualities required of a good upper-level functionary, including the ability to hold her own counsel and tell even her superiors only what she thinks they need to know. The picture of governmental bureaucracy given through her portrait reveals its cynicism. While Judith does seem sincerely to care about what happens to the American people, she also has no difficulty in using her concern about those people to advance her career. As the novel continues, she repeatedly reveals her ability to combine worthy goals and personal ambition, or, to put it another way, good ends and questionable means. Her covert control of Joshua and his family is what makes his mission possible and enables it to succeed. Her power increases as Joshua's influence grows, for she has successfully both promoted him and his mission and made that mission dependent upon her masterminding.

McCullough parallels Joshua and Judith in some interesting ways and balances them against each other. As his mental and physical conditions worsen, Judith's less admirable qualities become more apparent. She is forced to become ever more manipulative and to be increasingly direct and open in her control of his behavior and activities. Ironically, a moment of great triumph for Judith occurs when Joshua's decline is becoming clear. Her superior calls her by her first name and cynically compliments her success by calling her "the coldest-blooded bitch I've ever met" (319), which Judith accepts as an accolade. Her triumph is immediately undercut, however, in a sharply ironic vignette, for the Secretary sends away her car and leaves her to wait to catch a bus home. Her power is still dependent on others, on men, and her ambition still is not fulfilled.

As Joshua's sense of mission leads to madness, it causes Judith to demand recognition of her power, her responsibility in helping him succeed. When she confronts him with his Messianic obsession, she tries to shock him by pointing out how much of his success has depended on her efforts. "If there is any reason in the world why you are where you are and who you are on this day, that reason is *me! I* put you here, *I* created you! And I did not put you here to act out a second coming" (324), she screams at him. She is aware that she is losing control over the one man who has made possible her gathering of power, and she also sees the good that his inspiration of the people has brought. These contradictory emotions, along with the frustration which has grown as Joshua has refused to do as she wished, leads to her rare loss of emotional control.

A woman of decision, however, she acts quickly to remove Joshua so that he will not destroy his work and so that he can be cared for. As always, her plans are impeccable and should have worked. She is still the gifted manipulator. The problem is that those she counts on let her down, and the result is disaster. However, unlike Joshua, the man of feeling and thought, the woman of action is not harmed by the dramatic conclusion to the March of the Millennium. She is not able to prevent effects from Joshua's self-crucifixion which are undesirable from her point of view, but she does cement her own power. Ironically, she does this not as might have been expected by replacing her superior, who failed her and the President by being drunk at the crucial time. Instead, she does it by marrying the President. Thus this strong woman, who has always succeeded by her own ability and hard work, now reverts to the age-old stratagem of the helpless woman by seizing power in the person of a man whom she can control. On the one hand, then, this is a drastic change in Judith's behavior patterns. On the other hand, however, it is absolutely in keeping with her consistent grasping of power through whatever means seem most practicable. To the end, she remains a contradictory and fascinating character.

Few other characters require much analysis. Joshua's family, consisting of his widowed mother, two brothers and their wives, and one sister, is always present in the background. All are briefly portrayed, and the women especially are nicely distinguished from each other. Mama is a weak and rather silly woman. She never quite understands what is happening or what Joshua needs. She is goodhearted, but her lack of intelligence keeps her a rather useless person. The two sisters-in-law (one of whom is in love with Joshua) and the sister (who bitterly resents him and her servile position in the family) are also sharply depicted. The two brothers are not well individualized and never achieve much life. None of these family members plays a significant role in either plot or themes of the novel.

More significant because they have important functions in the plot are the President and Judith's superior, the Secretary of the Environment, and these two functionaries are drawn sharply if with broad strokes. They do not present a particularly pleasant picture of the government, for they seem to be motivated principally by cynicism and greed for power. The Secretary, a particularly weak man, is not very smart and cares only about himself. He is easily manipulated by Judith. His drunkenness at a crucial moment is well prepared for and completely within character. The President, who appears less often, is more likable. Mc-Cullough creates sympathy for him by using his unfortunate family situation, in which he behaves with dignity. He and his wife have the permitted one child, tragically a mentally retarded daughter, and for political expediency the President has used his influence to ensure that his wife will not be permitted the second child for whom she so desperately yearns. Her thwarted maternal cravings lead her into promiscuous and destructive behavior, which the President bears stoically. His wife has rejected their handicapped daughter, but the President loves her and spends what time he can with her. Through dramatizing this family tragedy, McCullough makes the President a man of admirable humanity.

Other characters briefly come to life in the pages of *A Creed for the Third Millennium.* Notable among them are Billy, the pilot, and Moshe Chasen, the Department of the Environment official who first identifies Joshua Christian for Operation Search. But Joshua and Judith are the only two essential characters of this long and complex novel.

THEMATIC ISSUES

Dystopian novels are by definition novels of ideas, generally political or social ideas. They ask "what if" and then follow out the consequences of the assumptions they have made. The themes of this novel cluster around two ideas: the particulars of the disastrous situation of the world in 2032 and the proposed solutions. On the one hand, the novel predicts certain outcomes of the international political situation of the mid-1980s; on the other, it studies the effects of climatic change. In neither of these cases, however, does McCullough really examine cause-and-effect relationships. She does not, in other words, tell readers how and why the world of 2032 became what it is. She simply imagines that world and then sets her characters to interacting within that world.

Some of the most interesting themes, or abstract ideas, of the novel obviously inhere in the characters. The depiction of Judith Carriol is particularly stimulating. A very complex character, she reveals conflicts of several sorts on several levels. One obvious thematic concern illustrated through her is the age-old question about ends and means. What she desires to accomplish is good, but her methods are manipulative and covert. The working out of the novel would seem to suggest that her evil means corrupt the good ends she has sought. As a woman, she illustrates social issues relating to the status of women and how they are able to accomplish their goals. A very unfeminine woman, who is both physically attractive and ambitious for power, she has risen, apparently through her own competence, to a position of authority when the book begins. In the course of the novel, she reveals herself to be a woman of great ability and cleverness. Yet Joshua Christian's mother, eager to see her son married and settled down, hopefully examines her as a prospective daughter-in-law, envisioning Judith's surrender to a domesticity which seems foreign to her nature. And when, at the end of the story, Judith finally achieves a pinnacle of power, it is not through her own accomplishment but rather through her marriage to an even more powerful man. Indeed, this marriage once again illustrates Judith's lack of concern about the means she uses to accomplish her ends as well as her capitulation to socially defined limitations on the roles of women.

The character of Joshua Christian raises issues of leadership and of what may happen to a leader who is adored, even worshipped. In his case, the result is madness, caused by the contradictions between his humanist message and the divinity ascribed to him by some of his followers and even at times by himself. There is an old adage that power corrupts and absolute power corrupts absolutely. *A Creed for the Third Millennium*, in the person of Joshua Christian, seems to suggest that, instead of corrupting, power sometimes destroys. He had meant to serve, but the adulation he receives so alters and confuses his sense of who he is and what he hopes to accomplish that his mind becomes unhinged. The power that he had exercised was unofficial, based on his charisma and on the need of the people for someone—anyone—who could bring them hope. When Joshua attempted to teach his message of acceptance, hope, and the old virtues, his overwhelming popular success was based mainly on his attractive personality and charisma and was thus shallow. His apparent power, misunderstood by himself and misused by others, leads him to disaster.

Others who are greedy for power, like Judith Carriol and her superiors (especially the Secretary of the Environment and the President), lack Joshua's purity of motive. Their manipulativeness and mixtures of motivations create a cynical portrait of politics and politicians. Their concentration on holding power and on protecting their own personal positions presents a sharply negative portrait of government functionaries and of the working of governmental agencies. Unlike some other aspects of conditions presented in the novel, the political structure of the United States in 2033 seems little changed from that of the 1980s. Only the existence of a Department of the Environment is a significant innovation, but that new Department operates much as any other governmental agency. And so the satiric study of its workings can easily be directly interpreted as a comment on the bureaucracy of the present.

Other themes are stated clearly by the situation and plot. Issues of overpopulation and proper means of population control are illustrated by the limitations on family size and the work of the Second Child Bureau. Questions are raised about how we might meet the challenge of drastic changes in our natural environment, questions very relevant today because of damage already done and continuing to be done by pollution. These rather specific problems, examined most fully in the novel's opening portions, are closely related to the genre into which this novel falls, the dystopia.

More subtly developed themes relate to the psychological and spiritual issues of the novel. In a society in which depression is both widespread and well motivated by actual conditions, what can be done to improve morale and enable people to live productive lives? This is the central question of the novel, and one possible answer is suggested: a humanly centered, nonreligious "creed," which does not depend on the existence or worship of a deity. "Millennial neurosis," the psychological ailment invented for the novel and in the novel described by Joshua Christian, defines the spiritual malaise of the book's imagined society. McCullough presents a world in which traditional Christianity has lost force and relevance, drawing to an obvious conclusion the loss in influence of the so-called mainline churches since the 1960s. Ironically, she uses their faith, apparently dead in the world of 2033, as the basis for the new faith she proposes. The virtues called for in the new creed of Joshua Christian, however, grow directly from the Biblical injunctions on faith, hope, and love, and it is primarily the suprarational characteristics of traditional religion, specifically faith in a personal God, that is denied. And yet the human yearning for something beyond the rational to believe in is illustrated in Joshua's tormented desire to be a new Christ, in the hysteria of his denials of any divinity, and by the widespread efforts made immediately after his death to ascribe supernatural powers at work through him.

Joshua's message and his mission present the novel's proposed solution—a rather simplistic reliance on positive thinking, looking to the future rather than to the past, and doing one's best. The conclusion of the book points out that such a message when conveyed by a charismatic person and climaxed by martyrdom, may turn into a new religion, or at least it will take on the superstitious trappings of a religion. In so doing it will be built on a lie. If it succeeds, it will be because of the power of the lie, and it will be based on the cult of a personality, not on the truth of the message.

AN ALLEGORICAL READING OF *A CREED FOR THE THIRD MILLENNIUM*

Allegory may be defined as a literary device in which elements within a story (characters, most obviously) are equated to events outside the story itself but assumed to be familiar to the reader. In reading an allegory, the reader is expected to be separately aware of both the symbolic elements and the things for which they stand. In using allegory, an author is constructing two plots at the same time: one is open and directly told and is simply the actual events of the story; the second is more subtle and concerns the abstractions or ideas for which the characters or allegorical elements stand. *A Creed for the Third Millennium* purports to describe the creation in Joshua's book of a new Bible, or at least a new New Testament in Joshua's book. The birth of Jesus opened the first millennium, since the Christian calendar used in the West began with what was thought to be the date of His birth. His life and death and the beginnings of the faith founded on His message, as told in the New Testament, became the foundation for a religion and for a way—or many ways—of living and relating to the world. McCullough suggests that the powerlessness of Christianity and the combination of new problems which come together at the beginning of the third millennium require a new faith to replace the old one. This novel describes the founding of that new faith, in the life and death of Joshua Christian, and it parallels the experiences and ideas of Joshua to Jesus in many ways.

Most of McCullough's major and many of her minor characters may be directly equated to individuals in the story told by the four New Testament Gospels, and the main outlines of the experience and action in the last year of the life of Dr. Joshua Christian parallel those of the three years of Jesus' ministry. Joshua was born at the end of the year which opened the new millennium, in December 2000 (98). He is about Jesus' age, but while Jesus' mission lasted three years, from age thirty to thirty-three, Joshua's begins when he is thirty-two and lasts for less than a year. He dies at the Biblical age of thirty-three, but his career has been dramatically foreshortened.

In addition, other parallels to the New Testament broaden the import of the novel to include Joshua's message and the lasting impact of his life, not just his simple biography. One very important reference is to the very famous passage on faith, hope, and love (sometimes translated "charity") in Paul's first letter to the Corinthians (1 Cor. 13:13). Those are the three qualities which Joshua aspires at the beginning of his mission to bring to people (149). At the end of his struggle, after his death, President Reece sums up Joshua's contributions as he announces Joshua's death. He says, "He was faith. He was hope. He was love. He has offered you a creed for this third millennium, a creed which is a restatement of the unquenchable spirit in Man and Woman, a creed which can offer all of you a positive and ongoing philosophy of life in the midst of this cold, hard, unrelenting third millennium" (444). In these words, the President makes explicit the connections between Joshua's and Jesus' stories. He equates the man with his message.

Joshua Christian's sense of mission and his growing identification of himself with Jesus Christ form the backbone of the action of the novel. Without that identification, his crucifixion of himself at the end would be pointless. A major way in which McCullough prepares her readers for that ending comes through the development of Joshua as a character and though his gradual but consistent change in the direction of obsession with God and with his mission. But she has also carefully set up her narrative to call attention to parallels between Joshua and Jesus. To begin with, there are the names. "Joshua Christian" obviously echoes "Jesus Christ." "Jesus" and "Joshua" are, in fact, different forms of the same name, and "Christian" is an adjective derived from the noun "Christ" and thus, of course, is the label attached to followers of Christ. Names of his family members continue the parallels. Joshua has brothers named James and Andrew, as did the Biblical Jesus. The women of his family, while not continuing the exact parallels, also echo names of familiar Biblical names: Mary, Martha, and Miriam. His mother's given name does not appear, but his long-dead father had been called Joseph, another exact parallel.

The parallels in naming continue outside the family. Two other names, one minor and one major, extend these connections. Joshua's ghost writer, the person responsible for committing his ideas to paper, is named Lucy Greco, an obvious play on the name of Luke (who was a Greek), the author of the third Gospel and of the Biblical book called "The Acts of the Apostles," which recounts the history of the early Christian church. Lucy is obviously not an exact parallel with Luke, but the similarities in name and function are clearly not accidental and they help to emphasize the presence of Biblical parallels as an important and repeating motif.

Finally, much more importantly, Judith Carriol's name echoes that of Judas Iscariot, the disciple who betrayed Jesus. Although Judas' name has become a synonym for treachery, scholars over the centuries have argued about his motivation, and some theories suggest that his betrayal was not the simple result of greed for the thirty pieces of silver. Judith, like that more complicated Judas, is a complex and many-sided character. She believes in Joshua's mission, as Judas may have believed in Jesus'. The actual nature of her betrayal, however, is less clear. Does it occur when she confronts him with his obsession? Or is it when she unintentionally sends him off to his death? In either event, she herself accepts that she has betrayed him. However, unlike the Biblical Judas, Judith comes out of this experience stronger. Judas committed suicide because of his guilt and remorse, but Judith solidifies her position by marrying power.

Other names, also Biblical but not Christian, complete this pattern. Three political figures are paralleled to powerful Romans whose actions have relevance to the Christian story. A former president, who never appears in the action of the novel but is referred to frequently as an extremely powerful man, rather in the mold of Franklin Delano Roosevelt (like Roosevelt, he served four terms), had been named Augustus Rome, usually referred to as Gus Rome. The current president is Tibor Reece. These names obviously echo the names of the Roman emporers Augustus Caesar and Tiberius. Additionally, the man who is Secretary of the Environment, a subordinate of Tibor Reece, is named Harold Magnus. "Magnus," Latin for "great," is one obvious clue that this functionary is intended to parallel Herod the Great, king of Judea during the life of Jesus and a vassal of the emperor. Other figures who might be expected (John the Baptist, Peter, Pontius Pilate, for example) are not present. McCullough did not attempt to create an exact copy of Biblical events or personages. But the collection of parallels which she did include is so obvious as to require that the reader examine the meanings which the events of the novel take on when seen in the light of the Biblical story.

Naming initially establishes the presence of Biblical parallels, but there are other kinds of Biblical references. Most prominent are incidents which can be referred to specific events recounted in the Gospels. For example, the incident of Jesus' feeding the multitude by multiplying a few loaves and fishes (Luke 9:10–17) becomes a metaphor when Joshua suggests that his book feeds the multitudes spiritually as the loaves and fishes had physically fed the crowd following Jesus (168). *God in Cursing* is specifically compared to the Bible in its phenomenal sales (194). The sending of Joshua's brothers to Europe and South America (278) parallels the sending out of the apostles to preach Jesus' message (Luke 9:1–6). Joshua is performing not many little wonders but one great miracle (281), and he illustrates his speeches with "little allegories" (288) or parables. He refers to his followers as "disciples" and tells them he is always with them (322; Matt. 28:20). The March of the Millennium, of course, is parallel to the triumphal entry into Jerusalem (Luke 19:28–39). The parallels multiply in the last sections of the novel, as Joshua becomes more and more caught up in the question of his identity and as McCullough hammers home his likenesses to Jesus.

Some parallels are quite precise, but others are more general, even vague. It is only after a reader begins following and looking for them that some similarities will be noted. Joshua's long speech, followed by questions and answers, when he appears on the late-night television show just before the publication of his book (246–64) may be equated to the Sermon on the Mount, which contains Jesus' central teachings. Several passages may be seen as resembling Jesus' agony before His crucifixion, and of course the crucifixion itself has meaning only as an imitation of Jesus' execution. McCullough does not follow the chronology of Biblical events, and she does not usually attempt any precise accuracy of detail. In fact, as we will see, the differences ultimately become of greatest importance.

Some elements of the Biblical story, which one might expect to be present, are significantly absent, and others are changed in important ways. Joshua's mother, far from a pure and holy woman, is basically rather stupid. There is no character like John the Baptist to foretell Jesus and His mission. Neither is there a single meal to serve as a last supper, or, as noted, a Pontius Pilate character to be the instrument of His condemnation and death.

In allegorically connecting Joshua Christian and the beginning of the third millennium to Jesus Christ and the beginning of the first, McCullough does not intend to say that Joshua really is a Christ-figure or that traditional Christian solutions are workable in the new situation of the twenty-first century. Jesus went knowingly and with acceptance to His death, but Joshua insanely and intentionally kills himself. Jesus was forced to carry His cross to the place of execution, but Joshua drags the cross he is constructing to the only place he can find to place it. Jesus is crucified before a crowd, but Joshua only imagines onlookers. Joshua echoes many of Jesus' last words, but these lines are ironic in this new context. Jesus' death has been understood as a political and theological necessity, but Joshua's is totally unnecessary, the result of a series of meaningless accidents. The New Testament and the Christian faith built upon it present the aftermath of Jesus's death—His resurrection—as bringing hope and meaning to human life. *A Creed for the Third Millennium* presents the aftermath of Joshua's death, the manipulation of public opinion by government and by naive followers of Joshua, as being built on lies and therefore meaningless. Joshua had died proclaiming himself (to no one) fully human and fearing that, since he was being seen as divine, his work was all in vain. The novel's conclusion suggests that he was right—but that a new edifice of superstition may be built on the "Christian myth" growing up around his life, work, and death. This allegorical reading suggests that perhaps the true new creed referred to by the title of McCullough's novel is the novel itself, not Joshua's book. Perhaps *God in Cursing* serves as the new gospel and *A Creed for the Third Millennium* as the new Acts of the Apostles.

The allegorical connections between McCullough's book and her sources in the New Testament and in Christian belief are important to any full understanding of the novel. It can be read simply as a dystopia which predicts a dire situation in the future and depicts unsuccessful attempts to cope with that situation. It can be read as a case study of a man, brilliant and charismatic, who tries to save his people and is too successful, resulting in his becoming obsessed and eventually insane. When the Biblical elements are added, it can be read also as a criticism of the supernatural elements of Christianity—or at least as a denial that Christianity can have any meaning or power in the third millennium. If there is to be a creed for that third thousand years, it may be based on the ideas of faith, hope, and love, and it may be forward looking, not nostalgic. But it would seem that it cannot be based on the personality and experience of an individual human being.

7

The Ladies of Missalonghi
(1987)

With her fifth novel, McCullough again attempted something new, although, as in *Tim, The Thorn Birds,* and *An Indecent Obsession,* her new book makes use of a number of the conventions of the romance form. As before, however, her use of the romance genre is unusual, and it criticizes the genre while employing familiar motifs taken from it. *The Ladies of Missalonghi* (1987) is set in Australia several generations ago and uses Australian landscape and social or cultural history. It centers around a female protagonist who gains strength and assertiveness during her experiences within the novel, and it concludes with a happy ending. But some aspects of both plot and character are distinctly unromantic in nature and complicate any interpretation of the novel as an example of that form. Additionally, ethical issues are raised by the novel—both by the history of its creation and by its working out of character and theme.

Several of McCullough's novels can be fully interpreted only by referring to phenomena outside of the novels themselves. For example, *A Creed for the Third Millennium* directs the reader's awareness to both Biblical materials and late twentieth-century social history, and the Roman novels treat actual historical events and people. *The Ladies of Missalonghi,* however, is different in that it bears a hidden relationship to another novel. Not long after its publication, McCullough was accused of plagiarizing a rather obscure novel, *The Blue Castle,* by the Canadian novelist, L. M. Montgomery. Parallels between Montgomery's and McCullough's works are clear, and a possible defense is that McCullough was actually parodying Montgomery and the sentimental and romantic fiction of that early twentieth-century Canadian writer. These accusations will be considered later. In addition, the behavior of McCullough's protagonist raises ethical questions. She succeeds in her quest for freedom and love, as is of course central to the book as a romance—but that success comes through deceit, and she is encouraged at the end of the novel to continue the lie. The ethical question is explicitly raised by the book, but the solution offered would not have been socially acceptable in the time of the novel's action—or, indeed, in the world of the sentimental romance in general. In fact, the novel may be read as an antiromance—a book which uses many of the motifs of the romance in order to undercut the genre itself by showing its absurdities and clichés.

PLOT DEVELOPMENT

Stripped to its essentials, *The Ladies of Missalonghi* is the story of a poor, young woman named Missy Hurlingford, living with her widowed mother and spinster aunt, who finds freedom, love, and wealth through marriage to a mysterious stranger. Stated this way, the novel may be seen as a retelling of the old Cinderella story—and indeed McCullough intended to write a modern version of the Cinderella tale. Her working title was "Cindermissy" (Anderson 285), which gives the game away, and she has called the book "my fairy tale" (Steinberg 110). The details in the story which reveal that origin can be easily observed and relate to both plot and characters. There is only one wicked stepsister here, Missy's beautiful cousin Alicia, but there is also a fairy godmother, the uncanny Una, who is instrumental in bringing together Missy and John Smith, the romantic love interest. There are also important differences between the fairy story and this modern tale. Missy's mother loves her, though she does not easily show it. Instead of a wicked stepmother, the "villain" is an extended family controlled by powerful men who exploit and cheat the threesome of Missy and her mother and aunt. John Smith does not romantically pursue Missy. In fact, it is she who determinedly pursues him, and she uses a lie to persuade him to marry her. The story concludes with depiction of their sexual fulfillment together, their confounding of the wicked family, the revelation of the identities of John

Smith and Una, and the explicit clarification of Una's function in bringing Missy and John Smith together.

The novel opens by dramatizing the poverty of Missy and her elderly female housemates and quickly introduces most of the book's important characters. Missy's love of reading romantic fiction is established, and Una is introduced. She is a distant relative, a newcomer to the town, who officiates at the local lending library, selects suitably sentimental novels for Missy, and encourages her first attempts to become assertive and independent. John Smith, a rough-tongued stranger, is also presented early, and although he is unlike the traditional hero of romance (too old, apparently too uncultivated, and too crude), his function in the novel is transparently clear. The engagement and approaching marriage of Missy's cousin Alicia forms an important plotline. Missy and Alicia are opposites in many respects. Like the cruel stepsisters of the fairy tale, Alicia sees no beauty or goodness in poor Missy and treats her with contempt.

At the age of thirty-four, Missy seems healthy but suffers from a recurrent "stitch" which brings on severe if usually brief episodes of pain, even to total collapse. These episodes are used to bring Missy and John Smith together and enable her to trick him into marriage. One attack renders her briefly helpless—he observes and carries her home, introducing them to each other in a more romantic way than their earlier brief and antagonistic encounter. After a medical examination, in which she learns that she has only a pinched nerve, not a serious heart problem, she steals a physician's report which states that its unnamed subject suffers from terminal heart disease and has no more than a year to live. Using this as evidence that he has little to lose in marrying her—and in spite of his repeated and firm refusals—Missy is able to persuade him to marry her and take her to live with him in his beautiful valley. And, of course, as the Cinderella story and the romance form both require, they then fall in love with each other and the end of the novel implies that they will together live happily ever after.

Concurrent to the romance plot, a combined economic and family plot is playing itself out. The nature of family relationships and the greed of this family are essential here. Missy learns that her male relatives, holders of all power and wealth in this oppressively patriarchal family, have been systematically cheating her mother and other women relatives out of income that should have been theirs and are now intending to wrest from them the shares of stock that had all along been producing the income they never received. Several plotlines, domestic and economic, come together very neatly here. Angered to learn that Alicia does not want her as a bridesmaid because her appearance would spoil the effect at her wedding, Missy furiously destroys the dress Alicia had patronizingly given her to wear to the wedding. Then, her wrath still not lessened, she goes to return the ruined dress—now smelling of manure—and overhears her uncle, Alicia, and other powers within the extended family discussing their plan to steal the stock from "the aunties." A few days later, accompanied by the always instrumental Una, she travels to the city for the previously arranged medical appointment which puts the useful, though dishonestly obtained, medical opinion into her hands. On that same trip, she sells the shares of stock her unscrupulous relatives had been attempting to acquire. In so doing, she brings financial security to the impoverished single women of the family, and she gives herself the opportunity to escape from her grim situation through marriage.

What remains is the depiction of the marriage of Missy and John Smith—unexpectedly blissful given the circumstances which created it, but not of course surprising to readers familiar with romance conventions. Their sexual union is frankly described. John Smith's first feelings of love for Missy are shown, as are his hopes that somehow their love can prevent the death from heart disease which he believes is her destiny. Questions of identity are also resolved, with the explanation of who John Smith and Una really are—as well as their former relationship to each other. She turns out to be the ghost of his dead wife, atoning for her guilt in life, and he is a rebellious and independently rich member of a prominent city family. Una, now with added authority because of these revelations, tells Missy to keep secret her lie to John Smith, and the clear indication of the novel's ending is that her stratagem will work, for he will believe that it is their love that has, in true romantic fashion, healed her.

CHARACTER DEVELOPMENT

Since they follow the model of the Cinderella tale, the characters in *The Ladies of Missalonghi* are patterned after conventional types used in the romance. Missy serves as the protagonist-heroine, the Cinderella figure, and John Smith, the stranger who seems both alluring and ominous because of his unknown past, plays the role of the prince. Their relationship, of course, is at the heart of the novel. There is some element of mystery about each of them—the full name of each is concealed until the conclusion—and, in fact, John Smith's true full name is never revealed.

Missy is always referred to by this obvious nickname. Indeed, when she visits the doctor in the city, his uncertainty about her actual name calls to the attention of the reader the fact that her name has never been clarified. Eventually, it is revealed that her true given name is "Missalonghi," identical to the name of the house in which she has grown up and which seems to be the source of the novel's title. John Smith is identified in three different ways. First he is the nameless stranger who gives rise to much speculation because outsiders are rare in this ingrown community. Then he is identified as John Smith, a name which seems patently false and fuels the rumors that he is a man hiding a terrible past. Finally his original first name, Wallace, is given but not his family name. All that is revealed about his original last name is that it was unusual and multisyllabic. He had legally adopted the name of John Smith, but his reasons were not of the nefarious kind suspected and bring no shame to him. His first wife had drowned and, though some had blamed him for her death, he was actually innocent of any wrongdoing.

Missy and John Smith complement each other in unexpected ways. The ugly duckling of her family, Missy is relatively short, dark, thin, undeveloped, dressed always in brown (which she hates)—a perfect example of a downtrodden girl waiting to be released into beautiful womanhood. She reads romantic novels and dreams of living in a beautiful valley adjoining her home. He is the stranger with the dark past, strong and with great resources (physically and financially), ready to have his faith in humanity restored by the love of a good woman. He is obviously a man of experience and not of visions, but he settles in the valley about which Missy had always dreamed. Missy is transformed into a vibrant woman, and John Smith's identity as a wealthy and generally benevolent man is revealed. The situational clichés are obvious. However, in a number of ways, John Smith's and Missy's characterizations veer from those suggested by the Cinderella tale. They are not completely the stereotypical hero and heroine of romance. Their lack of physical beauty and their ages alone, especially hers—she is thirty-four and he is around fifty—distinguish them from the conventional young lovers. And passionate as their love is at the end of the book, it remains built upon a lie.

Most other important characters are women, and several play significant roles in the structure of the novel and in Missy's growth. Two who play particularly important parts and who are contrasted with each other and with Missy are Alicia, her beautiful but mean-spirited cousin, and Una, her benevolent friend and fairy godmother (literally, her guardian angel). Una supplies her with new images for dreams, both in Una's own attractive and kindly self and in her lending of sentimental novels. To Missy, the idealistic reader of sentimental fiction, Alicia had personified the heroine of romance. She is engaged to be married to a very unromantic suitor (he is a relative who is many years her junior), while Missy is the perennial and fated old maid. Alicia lives in comfort, Missy in poverty. Alicia wears colorful and stylish dresses and shoes, while Missy wears a drab brown dress and boots. Alicia is self-centered and thinks only of herself, while Missy is lonely but truly concerned for the well-being of her mother and the other elderly women of her extended family. In an unexpected plot twist, Alicia throws over her intended marriage for a dramatically imprudent one. When events make the planned marriage no longer financially rewarding, she responds to the sexual advances of a chauffeur—he opportunistically gropes her breast—and she soon runs off with him. Her sexual awakening and elopement parallel and occur just after Missy's sexual awakening with John Smith. The difference is that the one is furtive and prurient, and the other is natural and liberating.

If Alicia and Missy contrast with each other on a number of levels as romantic heroines, Una and Alicia are contrasted in their relationships with Missy and in the roles they play in driving the plot. Alicia represents the wicked stepsisters and Una the fairy godmother. In plot, therefore, their functions are almost precisely the opposite. And their characters and relationships with Missy are similarly opposed. Alicia is malicious, delighted to show Missy up. Typical is her unthinking cruelty when she refuses to include Missy in her very large wedding party. Una, on the other hand, is kind and always goes out of her way to help Missy. She encourages Missy to act on her feelings, and—significantly—is always present when or just before Missy makes any decision or acts forcefully. She plants the ideas that inspire Missy to assertive action. Like John Smith, she is mysterious, a distant and previously unknown relative who has just come to town after suffering a broken marriage, a scandalous fact which sets her apart from the village.

Other characters of importance include the members of Missy's extended family. The Hurlingfords seem to comprise the entire citizenry of their village and its environs; John Smith and the doctor are the only non-Hurlingford characters of any significance. Missy's mother, Mrs. Drusilla Wright, and her aunt, Miss Octavia Hurlingford, the elderly sisters with whom she lives, are in some ways stereotypical examples of the elderly widow and old maid. They are not attractive, they appear to have no lives outside their meagre home, they are unable to show affection, and they accept their pitiful lot in life. Their trust in the unscrupulous males of their family is truly pathetic. This Cinderella story removes blame from the wicked stepmother and places it squarely on figures who do not exist in the fairy story—the father or father figure. Characterization, then, both follows and departs from the basic figures of the Cinderella story.

SETTING

Though setting may be most simply thought of as the place in which a work of fiction is located, it may include many other aspects of the background of a story. Not only geographical location and the physical features of the natural surroundings, but also climate or weather, human-made structures, even the atmosphere created by all these things may enter into setting. Time of the action may also be relevant. Several of these aspects of setting are significant in the setting of *The Ladies of Missalonghi*.

To American readers, perhaps the first point to be noted is the Australian locale. McCullough, because of the success of *The Thorn Birds*, is often thought of as a specifically or representative Australian author, and here she returns from her use of a futuristic United States in *A Creed for the Third Millennium* to the scene of her native land. The Australian background is indicated in a number of ways. Most obvious is the use of names of Australian places which can be easily located. Sydney is the big city to which Missy goes to consult a prominent physician and to sell shares of stock in a local company. The Blue Mountains and Katoomba, the town closest to Missy's fictitious village of Byron, are located to the west of Sydney, some distance inland. However, the Australian quality of the setting is not particularly striking. Similar villages and villagers existed in most backwaters of the English-speaking world in the general period of the novel. Little beyond the place names distinguishes them as specifically Australian.

In fact, the time of the action is a much more significant aspect of setting than is the country of location, though the two work together in important ways to set tone and ambiance for the novel. The time of the action, however, is less specifically indicated than is the place. It is never stated, and the reader must piece together clues which come largely from the daily lives of the characters. Hints are found in details of dress and manners as well as of technology. A motor car is a somewhat unusual phenomenon, but a chauffeur is involved in the action of later portions of the story, for example. Some readers may look for clues to the drawings by Peter Chapman which illustrate both hardcover and paperback editions. They show women in prim dresses of ankle length or longer and hats with wide brims. The attitudes of the characters—horror at the very idea of divorce, acceptance of powerfully patriarchal attitudes, social snobbery based on both wealth and family history—all coincide with placing the action of this story in the early years of this century.

Treatment of the landscape is not particularly Australian, and most of the novel could as easily be placed in the Canada or the United States of the period as in Australia. The dedication, to McCullough's mother, sets the tone: "For Mother, who has finally attained her dream of living in the Blue Mountains." This suggests that the Blue Mountains are symbolic of some sort of ideal place, a kind of Shangri La, perhaps, and the geographically illiterate reader might be forgiven for assuming they were mythical. The town of Katoomba is in the actual Blue Mountains, however, and so must be the presumably fictitious village of Byron. Few descriptions of actual mountains, however, are included in the novel. What is described is a valley within those mountains. That nameless valley, adjoining the house in which Missy lives, is her dream place, the real Shangri La of the novel.

The fictitious village got its name of Byron as a result of an obsession of the first Sir William Hurlingford, Missy's grandfather. McCullough refers to the "bizarre urban nomenclature" (20) which not only names the town for the poet of *Childe Harold* but also calls all other features of the town by Byronic names. This is not a tribute to Sir William's non-existent love of literature but the result of his pride in finding a poem that he could actually understand. George Street, Gordon Road, Noel Street, and Byron Street all immortalize the names of the poet. A particularly amusing name is Caroline Lamb Place, called after a woman who was passionately infatuated with Byron. Ironically, the street named for her is the locus of the town's brothel. This is no idyllic rural village. Its Hurlingford residents have either prospered as a result of inheriting property and cheating others out of their property (men and the women who have married them) or have become impoverished as a result of inheriting little and being cheated out of what little they had (women who did not marry well or who did not marry at all).

The final important aspect of setting is Missalonghi itself, the house in which Missy has grown up and where she lives with her mother and aunt. Named for the site of Byron's death, it is a dead-end place. The spelling of the name, as McCullough points out in a note preceding the text, is old fashioned ([ix]), appropriately to its function as home to three women, two elderly and one much younger in years though described indistinguishably from her elders in the novel's opening pages. The book, a maturation story as well as a romance, recounts her change from an old-appearing, unassertive, faded, disappointed creature, who has only unrealistic dreams to comfort her, to an assertive, vibrant, passionate woman. Though readers do not know until very near the end of the book that Missy's given name is actually Missalonghi, the full name with its associations with the death of a famous romantic poet seems most appropriate to the repressed figure of the novel's opening and the younger, even frivolous nickname more fitting to the free and spirited creature of the book's last pages.

THEMATIC ISSUES

Themes, or abstract ideas illustrated by the characters and plots of fiction, may include social commentary, as here in the depiction of the Hurlingford clan. Snobbishness connected to wealth and caste is satirized through the family's portrayal. The nature of the Hurlingford family underlines the time and social background of the novel's setting. It is sharply divided into haves and have-nots, with the have-nots being relegated to the sidelines of village activities. The patriarch of the family is Sir William Hurlingford, the third to bear that name and title, a reminder that the action occurs within the British Empire. Sir William's authority as spokesperson and supreme authority of the family is emphasized by his title as well as by the wealth which goes along with it, partly because of the peculiar inheritance customs of the family and partly because of the acquisitive behavior of two preceding Sir Williams. His dishonesty and total lack of scruples—he is the leader in the attempt to cheat Missy's mother and aunt and the other "aunties" out of their small inheritances—indicate how little such titles have to do with actual worth and reveal McCullough's critical attitude in this novel toward the social world of the Hurlingfords in backwater rural Australia in the early twentieth century.

The damaging effects of patriarchy (literally, rule by fathers) are demonstrated in McCullough's depiction of her central clan. The extended Hurlingford family is extremely patriarchal, a characteristic that has created men who are pompous and dishonest and women who are either pampered and shallow or deprived and powerless. The family has for several generations followed the practice of allowing most wealth and property to be divided among male heirs while females received only a small allotment of house and land. Unexpectedly, the result was to concentrate wealth in the hands of a few of the men and to leave those women who did not manage to marry well dependent on the good will—and honesty—of their male relatives. The rich condescend to and cheat the poor, and the poor, in the persons of "the aunties," struggle and scrimp and save and live sadly deprived lives. Drusilla and Octavia, the two elderly women with whom Missy lives, are both comic and pathetic, and Missy herself initially represents the powerlessness of women in a patriarchal society. McCullough's condemnation of such family structures is clearly seen in the pathetic strategems the elderly "aunties" are driven to in order to survive and the ways in which their personalities are wrapped by their straitened circumstances.

Contrasts between nature and society are thematically emphasized by the novel. Missy's valley becomes the place of the fulfillment of her dreams when she persuades John Smith to marry her. The valley is wild, unspoiled, untouched—ironically so, for it is only by inadvertance that the Hurlingford family has not taken title to it, as they have to all the surrounding land, and developed it. It is therefore a little oasis of beautiful and free non-Hurlingford property surrounded by commercialized, developed, spoiled Hurlingford land. The first description of the valley shows Missy pausing near it. She has been daydreaming, but now she actually looks at nature—its beauty and wildness are emphasized. What keeps it from being a complete refuge from the human pettiness of the town it adjoins are only a single wagon track that precipitously leads into it and the knowledge that the mysterious intruder, John Smith, is living there as a squatter. As she pauses by the entrance to the valley, drinking in its beauty, she suffers a recurrence of her "stitch" and is rescued and dramatically carried the short distance to her home by John Smith. Though they had met briefly in a village shop, this is their first significant encounter, and it is appropriately romantic.

The scenes depicting Missy's sexual awakening are set in the valley and contrast sharply with scenes in her house in the village. They occur first in John Smith's cabin in the valley and then outdoors, the morning after their first act of sexual union (which, unexpectedly for the genteel romance form, occurs after they agree to marry but before they are wed). That first act, occurring indoors, is not directly described, only John Smith's surprised pleasure in Missy's uninhibited response is shown. However, the outdoor scene which follows is explicitly depicted—his taking her first to his open-air toilet facilities and then to a natural basin fed by a warm spring where they bathe together naked and explore each other's bodies. The freedom found in the cabin and especially outdoors in the benevolent nature of the valley itself contrasts dramatically with the confinement of the village and of all the houses depicted in the village.

The profoundest, and at the same time most obvious, themes are the moral and ethical questions raised. These themes also relate to some of the most unsettling problems about the book. Secretiveness and, especially, deception, moral characteristics quite out of keeping with the usual romance world, are encouraged by the resolution of the plot. Missy wins John Smith through a lie. Una as a fairy godmother would be expected to speak for the value system encouraged by the novel. But having encouraged the lie in the first place, Una urges Missy to continue it at the book's end, to allow John to continue to believe that she suffered a serious illness when in fact she is perfectly healthy. Una's ethics in life had been questionable, but it is partly those very character flaws for which she is attempting to atone. Thus it may seem particularly odd that she exerts her supernatural powers almost entirely by encouraging her mortal protégée to be dishonest. The novel's happy ending, then, presents a marriage caused by manipulation, built on deception, and supported by a continuance of the original lie. By contrast, John's concealing his true identity is trivial. Romance readers anticipate a happy ending, but they expect it to be built on certain perhaps hackneyed moral values to which honesty and the full revelation of truth are basic. Those values are unsettlingly undercut by *The Ladies of Missalonghi.*

THE QUESTION OF PLAGIARISM

Not long after the publication of *The Ladies of Missalonghi* in 1987, startling allegations of plagiarism were raised against it and its author. In 1989 the Australian journal *Meanjin* published three articles presenting the case for plagiarism and discussing its implications. Gillian Whitlock discussed the nature of the argument about plagiarism and summarized the commonalities of the two novels; David Saunders analyzed legal implications; and Peter Anderson related the issues involved to certain is-sues in contemporary literary theory. McCullough's alleged source is *The Blue Castle* (1926), a novel by Canadian author L. M. Montgomery (best known for *Anne of Green Gables*). McCullough's novel is set in Montgom-ery's period rather than in her own, and similarities of both plot and character are striking. But differences in tone and resolution of plot are equally remarkable.

Whitlock has summarized the case against McCullough, listing a large number of concordances between the two novels. Some of these similar-ities are central to plot and theme, while others are quite minor. Most important, of course, are the basic plot and characters: both protagonists, Missy Hurlingford and Montgomery's Valancy Stirling (note the simi-larities in last names), are near spinsters who are much put-upon by acquisitive and hypocritical families. Both protagonists are romance readers and dreamers who have images of idyllic places where they set their reveries. Both live with two elderly female relatives, a mother and one other. Both are patronized or laughed at by the rest of their extended families, in both cases prominent clans dominating the villages in which they live. Each escapes to her longed for Shangri La—symbolically in Valancy's case and literally in Missy's—by persuading a mysterious man into marriage by telling him they have only a year to live. While *The Blue Castle* is set at the time of its writing, *The Ladies of Missalonghi*, writ-ten many years later, is set not in its own time but in that of *The Blue Castle*.

Striking as these similarities are, other resemblances seem particularly telling simply because they are so minor. Both Valancy and Missy are always dressed in brown, which they hate. Both despise the oatmeal which is a staple of their household diet. Each is flat-chested and dark, considered unattractive in contrast to a fairer cousin who is always beau-tifully dressed. In each case, that cousin is engaged to be married, while Valancy and Missy are presumed to have settled into spinsterhood. These parallels do not begin to exhaust the resemblances between the two books. It must be quickly obvious to a reader of both novels that the similarities are far too numerous to be coincidental. Two questions naturally follow: Are there significant differences between the two nov-els? And how are the similarities to be explained?

Some differences, while important in connecting the two novels to their respective authors, are in fact trivial. And some of the more obvious differences might be taken as revealing McCullough's attempts to cover her tracks. For example, Montgomery's novel is set in Canada and contains scenes which are much more sharply rendered and individual than anything in McCullough's book. And while Valancy's beautiful cousin might be seen in the role of the wicked stepsister, there is no character in *The Blue Castle* who fulfills Una's functions, no fairy godmother.

Two other differences, however, are crucial and relate to differences between the ethical behavior of the protagonists and between the tones of the two novels. Valancy Stirling really believes she has only a year to live. When she learns otherwise, she is distraught and tries desperately to free her husband from the marriage into which she has unwittingly tricked him. She is honest to a fault. Missy, however, consciously tricks John Smith into marriage and, at the end of her novel, is intent on keeping her secret. She is dishonest and manipulative. The tone of *The Blue Castle* is sentimental with comic overtones, while that of *The Ladies of Missalonghi* is often caustic and has elements of slapstick. Where *The Blue Castle*, not apparently a conscious effort at updating the Cinderella story, fits comfortably with the generally understood rules of the romance form, *The Ladies of Missalonghi* does not.

The accusations of plagiarism have been defended against in several ways, which are conveniently summarized by Whitlock. McCullough has acknowledged having read *The Blue Castle*, though she denied any very clear or specific recollection of it, implying that the similarities between the two books were a result of subconscious memory (Whitlock 271). Writers working within a genre with such clearly defined conventions as the romance, it is pointed out, will naturally recount the same basic story: young woman lives deprived life, falls in love with a mysterious stranger, and finds fulfillment with that stranger, who is revealed to be rich and powerful. The Cinderella tale is a version of that myth, and the romance novel tells and retells it, so it is not surprising that Montgomery and McCullough present readers with what, stripped to its basic essentials, is the same plot. Additionally, the settings for the two novels are similar. Though one is Canadian and the other Australian, both describe backwater, small towns or villages early in this century which were dominated by single families. This also, it is argued, helps to explain many of the parallels between the two romances. A village in southeastern Australia, it is argued, would be in many ways like a village in eastern Canada in the same time period. So readers should not be surprised to find some details of presentation to be similar (Whitlock 271).

These explanations—of unintended borrowing and of natural concordances resulting from generic conventions—do not, however, satisfactorily settle matters. The resemblances of *The Ladies of Missalonghi* to *The*

Blue Castle are so varied, so specific, and so pervasive as to seem necessarily more than echoes of a novel read long before and not consciously remembered. The same observation would seem to argue against easy acceptance of the defense which relies on similarities of setting. Neither explanation has satisfied readers of Montgomery, as Whitlock has pointed out, who feel that McCullough has "spoiled" the story (270).

A third explanation at first seems somewhat more compelling. This is the suggestion that *The Ladies of Missalonghi* is actually a parody of the romance form. Kate Grenville believes that McCullough's novel is a "spoof of the classic romantic fantasy" and points out the pervasiveness of "references to romantic writing [which] pop up everywhere like signposts" (Whitlock 274). Supporting this notion is the emphasis on Missy's reading of the sentimental romances supplied to her by Una. But this general explanation does not adequately justify the extensive unacknowledged parallels with one specific example of the form.

The extent of the similarities between Montgomery's and McCullough's novels, in fact, suggests that none of the relatively simple defenses against the charge of plagiarism is quite sufficient. The likenesses are simply too many, too precise, and too detailed. And some of those likenesses are so basic that treating one novel straightforwardly (Montgomery's) and one ironically (McCullough's) would require that there be important differences in the tone with which they are presented or in their resolution. For instance, Valancy and Missy have precisely the same romance reading habits, so differences in tone would be required to allow the reader to accept Valancy's reading as simply a part of the romantic world of her novel and to see Missy's reading as one aspect of parody of that same world. Such differences in tone do in fact exist.

Considering *The Ladies of Missalonghi* as a parody, not just of the romance genre in general but of Montgomery's novel in particular, would solve some of these problems, particularly that of the specificity and large number of echoes in McCullough's book, for then the heavy use of very exact echoes of *The Blue Castle* would be explained and justified as necessary to establish and carry through the parody. But for this explanation to be supported, there would need to be some evidence within McCullough's text leading to Montgomery. In other words, readers would have to be given some clues that would let them know that they were reading a parody and identify what precisely was being parodied.

An easy method of directing the reader's attention to *The Blue Castle* is found in Missy's romance reading. All that McCullough needed to do was to add clues there leading to Montgomery. One specific romance novel is described. Una tells Missy about _The Troubled Heart:_

> "It's all about a drab young woman who is utterly down-trodden by her family until the day she finds out she's dying of heart trouble. There's this chap she's been in love with for years, only of course he's engaged to someone else. So she takes the letter from the heart specialist telling her she's going to die to this young man, and she begs him to marry her rather that the other girl, because she's only got six months to live and after she's dead he can marry the other girl anyway. He's a bit of a wastrel, but he's just waiting for someone to reform him, only he doesn't know that, naturally. Anyway, he agrees to marry her. And they have six heavenly months together. He finds out that under her drab exterior she's an entrancing person, and her love for him reforms him completely. Then one day when the sun is shining and the birds are singing, she dies in his arms . . . and his old fiancée comes round to see him after the funeral because she got a letter from his dead wife explaining why he jilted her. . . . But he jumps up, wild with grief, rushes to the river and throws himself in, calling out his dead wife's name. And then his old fiancée throws herself in the river, calling out his name." (55–56)

Una's plot summary obviously is very close to _The Blue Castle,_ up to its melodramatic ending, and certainly sounds like a parody if only because it is so extreme. The title gives no clue as to what it might be parodying, and the plot ends differently from Montgomery's—and much more melodramatically. There is no clue leading specifically to _The Blue Castle._ In fact, if _The Troubled Heart_ is compared to Montgomery's work, it sounds more like the parodies of romantic and sentimental fiction which that author included in her best-known work, _Anne of Green Gables,_ in which she depicted the extravagantly melodramatic and pathetically sad romances Anne and her adolescent friends created in their "story club." Thus it is rather difficult to read this passage, which suggests her later actions to Missy, as a clue that McCullough's work is a parody of _The Blue Castle._

The Ladies of Missalonghi is not even consistent as parody of the romance genre. The resolution of McCullough's action and themes contains another contradictory element in the unmasking of Una. In the reading of the novel as a retelling of the Cinderella story, of course, Una serves as the updated fairy godmother. That is, she motivates and suggests the actions to Missy which enable her to play out her role as Cinderella. She is presented in a realistic manner—though from the very beginning, there are indications for the observant reader that Una is not quite—or just—what she seems. After finishing the novel, the reader can look back at the passages in which Una appears and observe that McCullough has actually played fair. The author has revealed information about Una's marriage, for instance, and has kept other characters offstage whenever Una and Missy meet. Nevertheless, the revelation that Una is actually John Smith's dead wife, who has come back to expiate her sins (of being a frivolous woman and a bad wife) by bringing Missy and John Smith together, is strikingly unexpected in a modern novel told in realistic language. The supernatural element simply does not fit with the rest of the novel's action and tone. The clues have not sufficiently prepared the reader, and the conclusion is jarring, balancing as it does the extreme and finally nonrational sentimentalism of the treatment of Una with the dishonesty of her final advice to Missy, that Missy never tell her husband the truth.

The question of plagiarism, or unintended borrowing, or parody of a specific novel, or parody of a genre, therefore, remains difficult to sort out. There are simply too many apparently contradictory elements which work against each other, with no single approach clearly predominating. We will see in the alternate reading which follows how this apparent confusion may be, if not resolved, at least made more defensible.

A DECONSTRUCTIONIST READING OF *THE LADIES OF MISSALONGHI*

Contemporary literary theory has introduced a number of related and interconnected theories and critical methods, which go by such names as "postmodernism," "poststructuralism," and "deconstructionism." The third of these has generally been the most fruitfully used as a tool for examining literary texts and will be the method primarily relied upon here. This group of theories may be most easily characterized by their reliance on linguistic theory, by their emphases on "differences," including those between the spoken and written word, and by their insistence that there are no final answers, no absolutes, when it comes to defining meanings. Among the thinkers most influential in establishing these approaches are Jacques Derrida, Paul de Man, and, in the United States, Jonathan Culler and J. Hillis Miller. For our purposes, the principal characteristics of the deconstructionist method to be noted are its comfort with the notion that a text can mean several things—or nothing—at the same time or, in other words, that a single text can support several different, even opposed, readings, none of which necessarily is "right." Just as much thinking relies upon opposites (think of our use of such clichés as "on the one hand" and "on the other hand" and our reliance on contrasting value judgments using "black" and "white"), a deconstructionist reading of a particular literary text may find opposite, apparently contradictory, meanings within that text. The term "deconstruction" is a blending of two words which carry opposite meanings, "destruct" (or "destroy") and "construct." While the first notion seems negative and the second positive, both approaches recognize the fact that texts—ideas, words, language itself—are creations (or "constructs"), not natural phenomena. The deconstructionist critic attempts to find the oppositions, the varied possible meanings, within a text.

Because of its tangled origins, *The Ladies of Missalonghi* is particularly suited to a deconstructionist approach. The question of plagiarism leads us into questions about what genre the novel actually belongs to, and answers to the question of genre imply markedly different conclusions about tone and meaning for the book. If the novel is a romance, a retelling of the Cinderella story, it depicts a woman coming to maturity and strength, finding fulfillment in love, and bringing prosperity to her loved ones through her newly assertive behavior. But we have seen that however much it may retain of the Cinderella story, it is at least equally dependent on Montgomery's earlier twentieth-century novel, another romance, from which it deviates in interesting ways. A deconstructionist reading allows us to balance the three principle readings—Cinderella story, antiromance, and parody (of Montgomery and of the romance form). All are valid, and yet each presents problems. Holding them all at the same time enriches and enlarges the meanings which are present in the work.

As a modern version of the Cinderella story, on the level of plot *The Ladies of Missalonghi* sets up a straightforward romance tale. Downtrodden young women with the help of her fairy godmother wins the love of rich and powerful man and ensures the comfort of the good women of her family. Idealistic and sentimental, this aspect of the story appeals to that in the readers which is comforted by formula literature with its

certainty of a happy ending. And McCullough gives her readers that happy ending. The presence of the supernatural, carrying the story of the world of fantasy, helps give the book the aura of romance.

But as antiromance, the novel at the same time undercuts the sentimentality of the romance form in which McCullough seems to be working. Her tone is realistic, even caustic at times. Neither Missy nor John Smith is the typical heroine or hero. Both have obvious flaws, and both are depicted too realistically, with all their weaknesses, to be the material of fantasies, unlike the usual central characters of romance. The moral questions raised by Missy's actions and by the resolution of the novel, which leaves their marriage built on both love and a lie, also undercut the insistence of the usual romance that love conquers all and that the heroine and hero merit that overwhelming passion because of their honesty. The tone of the ending is sardonic rather than idyllic.

The novel's ending, therefore, remains balanced between several radically different tones and meanings. "They lived happily ever after," as required by the Cinderella motif, is clearly implied. But that happiness will be built on a deception, and so the moral world of McCullough's world is quite different from that of the romance in general or of Montgomery in particular. And the sentimental treatment by Montgomery is consistent, while McCullough's text incongruously mixes realism and the supernatural.

As parody, *The Ladies of Missalonghi* is not just about love. It is also about writing, and it pokes fun at its literary subject, the romance. Whether read as either a parody specifically of Montgomery's *The Blue Castle* or generally of the romance genre, its subject becomes rather different from what most readers of romance anticipate, since it requires its readers to apply knowledge of a literary form, not just to fantasize about love. Of course, most readers, unfamiliar with the obscure novels of Montgomery and ignorant of the controversy over McCullough's use of her predecessor's work, would miss the elements of specific parody of Montgomery. But for those who recognize at least the parody of the genre, the complexities as well as the problems inherent in this text are enriched.

Additionally, it should be noted that language and tone also present problems that are relevant to these questions. McCullough's style here is generally simple, realistic, flat. At times, what have been referred to as her "cowpat jokes" (qtd. in Whitlock 269) jar against the world in which she has set her story. For example, it is unexpected to find a properly reared middle-class woman of the early years of this century using the expression, ''Bite your [or his] bum'' (54, 106), as Missy twice does. Even more surprising is the vulgar double entendre used twice in conversation between Una and Missy. First Missy does not understand why Una is amused when Missy, referring to her cousin William, says, ''Poor Little Willie is too limp'' (119), but after her sexual awakening she presumably understands when Una tells her that her marriage will succeed if she will ''[l]ook after his stomach and Little Willie'' (188). The differences in Missy's presumed knowledge here nicely dramatize her maturation, but they seem out of keeping with the world of romance. Here again two differing approaches seem to conflict with each other, the frank and realistic language comporting best with the parodic elements.

The Ladies of Missalonghi, then, may be read as a modern retelling of the Cinderella story, as McCullough has said she conceived it. It may also be read as an antiromance, a book which subverts the generally understood conventions of that form. Or it may also be read as a parody of the romance genre or of one specific romance, Montgomery's *The Blue Castle*. But none of those readings is completely satisfactory alone, for important elements jostle uncomfortably against each of these interpretations. As a deconstructionist critic would observe, the novel repeatedly undermines itself, with varied strands of its language, plot, characterization, and tone presenting oppositions to each other. Surprisingly, then, this rather simple appearing and brief book, based on an old and familiar genre and fashioned after a fairy tale, turns out to be much more complicated than many readers, brought to it by their knowledge of McCullough's Australian settings in *The Thorn Birds* or by their fondness of the romance genre, would have anticipated.

8

"The Masters of Rome" Series
(1990–   )

McCullough is notable for experimenting, for writing in a variety of forms. Commenting on her shift after *The Ladies of Missalonghi* away from fiction largely appealing to women readers, she observed that "at last I've written something that men won't be ashamed to be caught reading on the subway" (Steinberg 109). Her new project was something very different and extremely ambitious—a series of lengthy and detailed historical novels set in the closing days of the Roman Republic, approximately in the first century before the birth of Christ. Her earlier work in the historical vein had dealt with the relatively recent past, as in *The Thorn Birds* (or the even more recent past, in *An Indecent Obsession*) or, in the case of *A Creed for the Third Millennium,* with the imagined history of the future. While the time of setting is crucial for all three of these novels, none of them required meticulous historical research and none of them is primarily a study of its time. The series of Roman novels, which McCullough began publishing in 1990 and which she has referred to as "The Masters of Rome," takes the past itself as its principal subject. Her earlier books, stories of people who happened to live in a particular time and place, tell purely imagined tales. The Roman novels, on the other hand, are historically accurate stories of a particular time and place with actual people and events.

These novels are *The First Man in Rome* (1990), *The Grass Crown* (1991), *Fortune's Favorites* (1993), and *Caesar's Women* (1996), with one more novel planned to conclude the series. These books follow a coherent pattern, describe a connected series of historical events, use the same narrative methods, and depict many of the same characters (new ones are added and old ones drop out, of course, as the actual events dictate). Since the novels are projected to form one large whole and since they are so intimately interconnected, they will be treated here as a unit. The observations about the first four should, unless McCullough drastically changes her methods, hold true for the last. Since they are long and very intricate novels, the summaries here will of necessity be incomplete. They should, however, clarify the methods used by the writer and the effects achieved by the novels.

GENERIC CONCERNS

Historical fiction may be defined as any work set in the past. Loosely this may refer to any work set in a time earlier than that of its initial audience, but more specifically it is understood to apply to stories occurring before the author's life, requiring the author to research the time in which the story is set, not write from personal knowledge. As a result, two differing attitudes on the materials of the fiction are implied. There is the attitude of the characters in the story, which relates of course to the issues and problems of that time. There is also the attitude of the author toward those materials, and her or his attitude is of course shaped by the later time in which she or he lives and by the issues and problems of that later period. And, of course, the author creates the characters and depicts their attitudes. Particularly significant in this regard is the distance in time between author and materials and the amount of familiarity the audience may be assumed to have with the materials. An author writing about a recent past (for example, an author of the 1990s writing about the Vietnam War) may assume a relatively broad knowledge. But he or she must also assume that the emotions of readers may already be engaged in one way or another and thus that there will be certain strong preconceptions, either right or wrong from the author's perspective, which must be combatted or used. An author writing of a time in the more distant past or of a period with which the expected audience will have little familiarity has both an advantage and a disadvantage. There will be fewer preconceived ideas to combat, but much more background information will need to be given, forcing the author to risk burying the story in historical and factual data.

In writing about classical antiquity, McCullough chose a period very distant from her own time. Moreover, the period within classical antiquity is one with which readers have relatively little familiarity although they may assume that they know more than they really do. This series concerns the period of the collapse of the Roman Republic, a period just before that with which there is greater present-day general awareness. Twentieth-century readers are familiar with the periods of Julius and Augustus Caesar, largely because of their—generally superficial— knowledge of Shakespeare and the New Testament. However, McCullough's fiction leads up to these events, though a young Julius Caesar's apprenticeship makes up an important plot in *The Grass Crown* and *Fortune's Favorites.* His mature career is intended to climax the series.

Historical novels may be classified according to the kinds of uses they make of their materials. These uses vary from the quite loose to the extremely faithful. Some historical novels earn the name "historical" largely because they are set in the past and pay close attention to accuracy of setting—careful depiction of living and social conditions, for example, with little or no use of historical events and little or no portrayal of actual personages. *An Indecent Obsession*, considered as an historical novel though it depicts a period within the author's lifetime, fits into this first category. The other extreme consists of novels that follow actual history and make real historical figures their central characters. These books may be fictionalized only to the extent that they imagine motivations for their characters and create conversations and events to explain and make real and understandable the history they explore. McCullough's Roman series obviously fits into this latter category. The thoroughness of her research has often been remarked upon, and the extent of her coverage of her period and the number of actual characters she introduces are both strengths and weaknesses of her work.

Historical novelists following in the path of Sir Walter Scott, the greatest and best-known practitioner of the genre, often invent for their major plotlines stories about created characters who become involved in historic events and meet actual historical figures. Historic events do not often shape themselves into tidy and satisfying wholes, with beginnings, middles, and ends, which most writers and readers demand. So the central interest of the fiction may be structured by the author around an invented story, giving a form of the author's creation to the novel. Historical events and personages, which cannot be so easily manipulated as the invented ones, while important are not the source of the form or organization of the novel. McCullough does not use this method. Instead, she takes the historical figures as her central personages and the actual events as her main plots. The rare invented characters are minor ones who exist at the fringes of the basic plotlines. Since her important characters are real people and her purpose is to interpret and explain their actions, the reader may have difficulty distinguishing between the actual person and the literary character. In this examination, it is always to be understood that what is being discussed are McCullough's characters, her particular presentation of them, her forming of the historical events, and her selected and invented details. Thus we will be looking at this very intensely historical writing almost entirely as fiction.

One frequent criticism of these novels as novels is that they contain so much detail that the reader may lose track of plot and characters among the facts about military campaigns and political arguments in the Roman Senate. This profusion of detail is only one of the obvious ways in which McCullough's research shows itself. All three novels are accompanied by extensive apparatus, that is, material extraneous to the novel proper which is appended both to help the reader make sense of the story and to indicate the author's faithfulness to facts. Each novel contains, after the main text, an extensive glossary, rewritten to some extent from novel to novel. These glossaries explain many social and political phenomena which might not otherwise be made clear in the narrative itself. Latin terms, when left untranslated in the novel, are often translated and clarified in the glossaries. Sometimes particular historical interpretations which McCullough has chosen to accept, especially when these go against the usually accepted ideas, are explained in the glossary. Other helpful supplements include maps of the city of Rome and of various areas where military campaigns take place. These maps, as well as the portraits of characters, taken from actual statues, were drawn by McCullough herself. *The First Man in Rome* and *The Grass Crown* open with lists of characters, arranged by families. *The First Man in Rome,* after its glossary, contains a list of names with pronunciations indicated. *Fortune's Favorites* opens with a relatively full synopsis of the events of the preceding two novels as well as of events occurring between books. Its back endpapers give a chronological listing of historical events prior to the opening of *The First Man in Rome.* All three novels contain short notes by the author commenting very briefly on her research and uses of sources. These materials are helpful to the attentive nonhistorian reading the novels, and they underscore the importance McCullough has placed on thorough and accurate uses of historical fact.

PLOT DEVELOPMENT

The Roman novels contain several sorts of plotlines, which intersect and interconnect in a number of ways. These plots may be classified into three types: political, military, and personal. The same male characters are involved in all three types of plots, with the political and military plotlines being developed in great detail. By the political plot is meant the struggles for power within Roman society, especially within the Senate, in the period beginning in 110 B.C. These struggles sometimes spread out beyond the purely political arena and combine with the military plots. That is, in addition to wars against foreign states and peoples, civil wars between competing individual Roman leaders or groups are part of this history. For example, in *Fortune's Favorites,* Sertorius, a Roman, fights with Pompey and Metellus Pius, representatives of the Senate, for control in Spain. Finally, the personal plots concern the family lives of the men who are involved in the political and military struggles of the time. Their wives, children, and household slaves, who have no part in the political or military activities of the day, play important roles in these personal stories. For many readers, the personal plots are doubtless of greatest interest. Rinzler commented, in fact, on "the odd and unsatisfying alternation of gripping sections with others that make one's eyes glaze over" (19). The personal plots contain the bulk of those "gripping" passages, which contain the most human interest, are most recognizable to us today, and are least confusing because it is easier to keep their characters straight. Two of the most striking and interesting characters of the series are women who, of necessity, appear only in the domestic plots.

The series thus far is structured around the careers and shifting relationships of four main characters. *The First Man in Rome* is Gaius Marius's book, although Lucius Cornelius Sulla also plays an important part in it. This first novel of the series is the story of Gaius Marius' coming to power. In *The Grass Crown* Gaius Marius is eclipsed by Sulla, his former protégé, and dies angry and embittered. *Fortune's Favorites* dramatizes Sulla's physical decline and his greatest moments of power. It also focuses on what at first seems a trio of young men who represent the coming generation: Young Marius (Gaius Marius' son), Gaius Julius Caesar, and Pompey Magnus. Just as Marius and Sulla had been contrasted with each other, so these three young men are made to represent varying attitudes. The two women who are carried through the novels in important roles are Julia, Gaius Marius' wife; and Aurelia, Gaius Julius Caesar's mother.

The methods by which these stories are told are largely quite conventional. A straightforward chronology of events is generally used, although sometimes when events at different places overlap with each other in time, the narrative will backtrack in order to catch up. Sometimes there are flashbacks, as when a new character is introduced and his (and it usually is a male) background and political and social alliances need to be clarified. The narrative is a very traditional third-person omniscient method (that is, all characters are referred to in the third person, as "he" or "she," by the author, who reveals what characters are seeing, thinking, and feeling as well as what they are doing). However, letters from one character to another or from one characters to the Senate are often employed to move the action along. This epistolary (or letter) technique is used particularly frequently in earlier portions of the series.

In *The First Man in Rome,* chapters are entitled "The First Year," "The Second Year," and so on and are headed both by the date of the year (or in a few cases, years) and the names of the two men who then served as consuls. The novel covers the period from 110 B.C. to 100 B.C. Rome has become a world power, but it is still a city-state surrounded by peoples of other ethnic groups, many of them Latin speaking but ineligible for Roman citizenship. Gaius Marius, a rich man and a skilled military leader but an outsider, marries Julia and thus allies himself with a powerful and ancient but now relatively impoverished family. Sulla, poor and corrupt but from an ancient and respected lineage, kills his mistress and stepmother who stand in his way and denies Metrobius, his male lover and the only person he really cares about, in order to become a protégé of Marius. He marries Julilla, Julia's younger sister who had given him a grass crown, and thus cements the relationship between the two men. Marius and Sulla wage and win a war in Africa against King Jugurtha, and Martha, a Syrian prophetess, predicts Marius' great future power. The next threats come from the north and west, and Marius and Sulla campaign against the Gauls, whom they also defeat. Marius' marriage to Julia is happy, but Sulla's to Julilla is doomed from the start. When she catches Sulla making love to Metrobius, she kills herself. He remarries.

The Grass Crown, which simply numbers its chapters, covers the period from 98 B.C. to 86 B.C. Marius and Julia travel to Anatolia, where he involves himself in the complex politics of the region, temporarily defusing King Mithridates' plans for world conquest. Disagreements over the eligibility of Italians for Roman citizenship lead to war between Rome and the various city-states and peoples of the peninsula. Sulla, who had been in Spain, fights Mithridates, who is again trying to extend his power in Asia Minor. His adored son by Julilla is with him, and a softer side of Sulla emerges in their relationship, but the boy unexpectedly dies. Marius' and Julia's son, Young Marius, however, prospers. Continued military campaigns in Italy and Asia occupy much of the novel, and much brutality is depicted. Rome prevails but is weakened, and near chaos results. Gaius Marius seizes power, and a bloodbath follows. Declining into insanity, Marius appoints Gaius Julius Caesar, his young nephew, to serve as *flamen Dialis*, priest of Jupiter Optimus Maximus, in which position he is surrounded by taboos making it impossible for him to become a soldier. Thus he cannot look forward to a military or political career. Then, suffering the third of the strokes that have debilitated him, Marius dies.

A hiatus of three years occurs between the events of *The Grass Crown* and *Fortune's Favorites,* which a number of reviewers have called the best novel so far in the series. Oddly, some important historical events took place in that internovel period. At the end of *The Grass Crown,* the generalship of an army to fight against King Mithridates had been a central issue, but when *Fortune's Favorites* opens, that campaign had already been concluded. In *Fortune's Favorites,* in which chapters are headed by numbers but also indicate the years they cover, the action spans the period from 83 B.C. to 69 B.C. Three young men seem to be taking center stage; their rivalry replaces the one between Marius and Sulla which had propelled the first two books. However, Young Marius, having taken the wrong side—against Sulla—is soon killed, and Pompey and Julius Caesar are left to contend with each other. Sulla remains a powerful figure, though he is debilitated by a horrible but unnamed disease, his former beauty destroyed. He declares himself Dictator of Rome, and, as such, wields supreme power, ruthlessly destroys enemies, and brings both financial and political order. He retires to the countryside and a dissolute life with his last wife, whom he does in his fashion love, and with Metrobius. His death seems almost anticlimatic. Meanwhile, Pompey, a very young man whose arrogance leads him to adopt the nickname "Magnus," the Great, suffers humiliation and defeat and then finally prevails in battle against Sertorius, a disillusioned Roman, in Spain. Caesar, who has been released from his priestly function, succeeds in everything he touches. His relationship with King Nicomedes of Bythinia, who becomes almost a doting grandfather figure to him, enables him to bring that king's country under the control of Rome.

Then intervenes an unusually compressed and complete subplot, the story of the so-called slave revolt led by Spartacus. Most subplots in these novels skip through many pages, even several books, as the life story of a particular character is picked up at a number of different points. The story of Spartacus, however, is told within the space of about fifty-five pages near the end of *Fortune's Favorites*. Like the interrupted stories of many other characters, this plot diverts attention from the main players and is engrossing for its own sake. The doomed rebellion is recounted with sympathy for Spartacus, a character who goes through much change and development in his short and violent life. Because this highly dramatic, and emotional plot occurs shortly before the end of *Fortune's Favorites*, there is some danger that the following eighty-eight pages will be anticlimatic. McCullough uses those concluding pages to knit together strands from political and personal plots, connecting them to the partly military plot of the Spartacus story. Caesar shows his political skill by repeatedly acting as negotiator between Pompey and Crassus (co-consuls and rivals and recent victors, Pompey over Sertorius in Spain and Crassus over Spartacus in Italy). Premonitions and hints foreshadow *Caesar's Women*, and this book concludes, in a touching use of personal plot. First Julia, Caesar's aunt and Gaius Marius' widow, dies, and Caesar gives her an official and very public funeral, using the event to rehabilitate Marius' memory and to bring an official end to the era of his life. Then Caesar's young wife dies in giving birth to a stillborn child. Grieving, he sets off for Spain, and the novel ends.

SETTING

Setting, or the place and time in which a work of fiction occurs, is obviously of prime importance in these historical novels. They range widely over the known world of the period of the late Roman Republic. Much of the action occurs in Rome itself, which is fully depicted, even to the point of including much data about the daily lives of people of various classes. We learn how Roman apartment houses were laid out, how order was maintained at important crossroads, how slaves were managed, how women's dowries were negotiated, and a host of other details. Religion, including the varieties of gods and goddesses and the worship of those deities, is depicted. Social custom, such as who would be included and how they would be seated at dinner in a patrician household, is portrayed.

The events take characters to northern Africa (what was called "Africa Province"), Asia (Asia Minor, including "Asia Province" and other nations in what is now Turkey), Greece, Germany, France, and Spain. Italy, outside of Rome, is crucial in much of the action, especially in *The Grass Crown,* and the relationships of Italy and Italians with Rome and Romans form an important strand, changing from hostility and exclusion to inclusion. McCullough's research enabled her to be very exact in her description of landscape, the location of roads and even goat tracks, which may serve as roads in an emergency, and the layout of city walls and other defenses. She is as detailed in her depiction of North African and Oriental courts and rulers (the retinues of Kings Jugurtha, Mithridates, and Nicomedes, for example) as she is in her portrayal of the household of Gaius Marius and Julia in Rome. In fact, one of the principal observations a reader must make of these novels is the amount of detail they include. These are not short novels (781, 815, and 804 pages, respectively, not including the extensive glossaries but including some of the other supplementary material such as maps and portraits), and it is the fullness of detail in creating the place, the society, and the events that stretches them out to these great lengths. Many long passages, particularly in the military plots but also in the political sections, read like dry history texts of the sort that pile up facts without relating them clearly and meaningfully to the broad sweep of history, to their actual importance. Readers may often find themselves wondering exactly why particular leaders or armies are fighting each other. The meaning of the history and the connections of cause and effect are sometimes lost in the details.

CHARACTER DEVELOPMENT

Both a strength and a weakness of these Roman novels is their large number of characters. Many are portrayed effectively, and their stories create a living and vivid gallery. However, there are such a larger number of stories and people that the reader is often hard put to keep them straight. This difficulty is compounded by the complex and confusing naming system of the Romans. When every member of a particular branch of a family has two names in common, and when families limited themselves to a small number of what we would call given names, individuals are easily confused with each other. The confusion is made even worse by readers' desire to identify characters with which they claim some familiarity through knowledge of Shakespeare's *Julius Caesar* and *Antony and Cleopatra* or such films as *Spartacus*. Each time a Julius Caesar or Brutus or Cicero (whatever other names he may bear) turns up, one wonders if it is *that* Julius Caesar or other familiar character. The sensible reader will simply disregard these impulses and concentrate upon the stories of the major characters. The identifications will eventually become clear.

The First Man in Rome is largely Marius' book, though it introduces the rivalry with Sulla which underlies both it and *The Grass Crown*. In the first novel in the series, he is most generally presented favorably, though the seeds of the overweening ambition which will ultimately destroy him are present from the beginning. He is a rich man but unable to advance because his background is not of suitable Roman antiquity, and thus he lacks respect in this very class-bound society. He is a "New Man," a scorned outsider whose wealth is not of ancient Roman origins. An ambitious man, he quickly seizes an opportunity to overcome this disqualification when marriage with a woman from the most ancient and aristocratic family is offered. The fact that he is already married is slight impediment, and his easy divorce from his existing wife demonstrates both his ambition and the low status of women in this society. The fact that his marriage of convenience turns out to be a roaring success may seem rather surprising, but it reveals the good sides of Marius and particularly of his wife, Julia.

Throughout the novels, Marius is inspired by a prophecy of success beyond the wildest hopes of even a man of his wealth and military prowess. Martha, a Syrian prophetess, tells him,

> "Yours is a great destiny. . . . What a hand! It shapes whatever it puts itself to. And what a head line! It rules your heart, it rules your life, it rules everything except the ravages of time. . . . But you will withstand much that other men cannot. There is a terrible illness. . . . But you will overcome it the first time it appears, and even the second time. . . . There are enemies, enemies by the score. . . . But you will overcome them. . . . You will be consul the year after this one just beginning, which is to say, next year. . . . And after that, you will be consul six more times. . . . Seven times in all will you be consul, and you

> will be called the Third Founder of Rome, for you will save
> Rome from the greatest of all her perils!" (230; all but the first
> two ellipses are in the original)

Other details follow—especially that his wife's nephew will be even
greater than he. Marius, exemplifying the reliance on omens and proph-
ecies of the time, is deeply impressed by this prophecy, which both lays
out in brief much of the plot of the first two novels (and implies that to
follow) and motivates much of Marius' behavior in years to come. Even
when out of favor, he is certain that he will return to power, always
relying on those seven times as consul which Martha had promised him.
His two strokes incapacitate but do not defeat him, for the prophecy is
still incomplete. At the end of his life, he tries to nullify the final prediction, forcing his nephew Julius Caesar into a priesthood which makes
it impossible for the young man to enter the military and political career
which alone would enable him to outstrip Marius. The prophecy obviously connects with the title of the first novel in the series, for it is in
fulfilling the prophecy that Marius changes from being a "New Man" to
being the "First Man in Rome."

Marius is a moving force in all three sorts of plots—military, political,
and personal—as long as he lives. In the military plots, he is generally
triumphant. A brilliant tactician and a good leader of men, his wartime
triumphs are frequent. In the political plots, his record is more checkered,
but he is generally successful here, too. In his private life, he is mostly
exemplary as well, but much of this may be credited to Julia, his wise
and loving wife. Successful beyond almost all expectations, he of course
has many bitter enemies, and in the custom of the day he deals harshly
with them, but until near the end of his life, when he is sinking into
madness, he rarely shows the brutality so characteristic of his society.
His last days sadly contrast with his generally humane behavior, for he
descends to the cruelty and butchery of his opponents. Making young
Julius Caesar a priest is a final action of unparalleled selfishness, since
it destroys future opportunities for a young man who had been a second
son to him simply in order to protect his reputation from eclipse. This
act is also foolish. After depending on the accuracy of the Prophetess's
prediction in all details—and seeing even the most impossible clauses
come true—he now tries to prevent one final prediction from coming to
pass. The great man who has saved Rome by his military skill and his
political wisdom has degenerated into selfish cruelty. The contrast between the vigorous, mature man met in the opening pages of *The First*

Man in Rome and the senile, even insane, petty, and cruel old man who dies near the end of *The Grass Crown* is striking but well developed and clearly motivated.

For Sulla, introduced and fully characterized in *The First Man in Rome* and central to *The Grass Crown,* another symbol serves as motivation and gives the title to the book which revolves primarily around him. An extremely rare honor, a grass crown was a wreath made from grass and given to a military leader by his men after he had saved them and won the victory in battle. As with Marius and his prophecy, Sulla's promise of the grass crown comes to be a motivation before the event and later affects much else that he does. A young woman, eventually to become his first wife, idly weaves and gives to him a grass crown without knowing what a real one would mean, and he takes that as a prediction of later events. Long under the tutelage of and overshadowed by Marius, he finally does win a real grass crown, which he treasures and which seems to him to justify much that he does—and he behaves with unparalleled cruelty and brutality.

His character is complex and full of contradictions. Coming from an old and aristocratic family, he is born to poverty and grows up corrupt. He educates himself and loves the theater. Always totally self-centered, he uses and manipulates people skillfully. He murders close associates with impunity and slaughters enemies with a brutality which is striking even for this cruel world. When introduced in *The First Man in Rome*, he is living with two women who are identified as his stepmother (who is also his mistress) and his mistress, but when they stand in his way, he kills them both. These are only the first of a number of secret killings he will commit, always with the motivation of removing someone whose existence has become inconvenient to him. In *The Grass Crown*, he divorces a wife who had always bored him simply because she makes a remark that annoys him, using her barrenness as his pretext. He loves only two people. One is his son who dies young, in *The Grass Crown*, taking with him the purpose that Sulla had begun to find in life. The boy is the only person he ever cares for unselfishly. The other person he truly loves is Metrobius, the Greek actor who, though absent for long periods, is the one constant in his life. Sulla is a practicing bisexual from the beginning, using sex with women—or men—for his own benefit but always yearning for Metrobius. When his relationship with Marius is forming and he sees possibilities of advancement, he renounces Metrobius, but his longing for the actor never leaves him, and they occasionally meet in the years to follow, usually innocently. It is one such meeting, in which they resume their affair, that leads to the suicide of Sulla's first wife, Julilla, in *The First Man in Rome*. Near the end of his career, in *Fortune's Favorites*, Sulla makes Metrobius promise to come to him when he retires as Dictator. Metrobius agrees, and the result is a strange ménage, consisting of Sulla, Metrobius, and Sulla's last wife, which carries on a hedonistic and scandalous life in retirement.

Sulla's public life is as corrupt as his private life. He serves as Marius' second in command and loyal supporter as long as he can learn from him and profit by doing do. Then he becomes Marius' most fervent rival, and their enmity controls much of the action of *The Grass Crown*, when Sulla is in the ascendancy and Marius' position fluctuates. Sulla is totally ruthless. It must be admitted that all the Roman military leaders, as well as their enemies, are brutal to a degree that is horrifying to a modern reader. Sulla's fondness for having his defeated foes beheaded and their heads displayed in token of his triumph is notable, but even more generally admirable characters like Marius and Caesar indulge in such behavior. Sulla, however, carries his bloodthirstiness to a greater degree than do they, and his fondness for private murder to advance his public life is far beyond that of any other character.

Paradoxically, however, he is not a representative of total evil. He appears to love Rome, and he sometimes seems to act from patriotism rather than self-interest. He marches on and conquers Rome in an extreme act of defiance in *The Grass Crown*, and in *Fortune's Favorites* he declares himself Dictator. In each case, he acts swiftly and punitively against his enemies, but he also enacts sound and wise legislation, intended to stabilize a troubled city. As Dictator, he never intends a permanent seizure of power, and he retires when he believes his work is done, enabling the city to revert to the legal government.

Sulla might remind McCullough's faithful readers of Luce in *An Indecent Obsession*. Both characters are sexually ambiguous, manipulative, immensely self-centered, and physically beautiful. Both in large measure represent evil. And each is powerfully and effectively portrayed. The difference is that Sulla has a complexity lacking in Luce. Sulla contains some good; there is something he believes in—Rome. There are two people he loves—his young son and Metrobius. He does occasionally take actions for the good of something or someone outside himself. None of these statements can be made of Luce, who more purely represents malice and evil than does Sulla. Corrupt though Sulla may be, his surprising if occasional moments of nobility do add some small redemption to his character. McCullough's interpretation of him both makes him an engrossing fictional character and explains his place in history.

The other two male characters of principal importance are Pompey the Great (Pompeius Magnus) and Julius Caesar. They are members of the younger generation following Marius and Sulla, and their rivalry seems in some ways to echo that of their elders. Just as Marius was basically a sympathetic character and Sulla unsympathetic, so Caesar is favorably presented and Pompey unfavorably. But just as Marius is flawed and Sulla contains unexpected virtues, so too are Pompey and Caesar presented as complex and fully rounded characters. Both young men are occasionally compared to Sulla, continuing strands set up in the earlier rivalry.

Both younger men appear first in *The Grass Crown*, Pompey as the loyal son of a father brutally killed and Caesar as the nephew and aid of an ailing Marius. Members of Caesar's family and Caesar himself have played more prominent roles in the action of the earlier two novels, and so he is better known to readers than Pompey when *Fortune's Favorites* opens. As with the earlier two novels, the titles suggest content, and both Pompey and Caesar (along with several other characters) are frequently referred to as lucky, as blessed by the goddess Fortune.

Pompey has more to learn and sometimes seems to change more than Caesar, who is presented as almost startlingly bright and competent and successful. Both are physically beautiful and aware of their physical advantages. Pompey is arrogant and excessively sure of himself, irritating and amusing others by having given himself the nickname of "Magnus" (the Great) without having accomplished anything to merit the label. He feels an absolute certainty of success in battle and is shaken deeply when his first military encounters end in humiliating defeat. However, he does learn from his defeats and becomes a good general. In politics he behaves like a spoiled child when he is thwarted. He is petulant and demanding, always insisting on the honors he—often mistakenly—thinks are due to him. He sometimes becomes an object of jokes because his demands are so ridiculous. Caesar, on the other hand, always seems to justify his overweening certainty of success. When kidnaped by pirates, he persuades them that he is worth a higher ransom than they had intended to demand and blithely teases the pirate leader that he will capture and crucify him. When ransomed, he makes good on his promises, locating the pirate's hideaway by the simple expedient of having counted the number of coves they had passed on their way to it. He then fulfills his promise of crucifying the pirates, because he had given his word to do so, angering a provincial governor dismayed by the unnecessary loss of money which could have been realized by the sale of the pirates into slavery. The brutal side of the age is emphasized by Caesar's refusal to allow the pirate's legs to be broken when put on the cross, thus ensuring a long, slow, tormented death. Even Caesar, a man of his word, a good family man, a man of charm and apparent humanity, does upon occasion act with unnecessary cruelty.

Other—many other—male characters' lives and personalities are interwoven with the experiences of these principal players. Among those which are particularly striking are Quintus Sertorius, the loyal Roman who becomes the leader of a Spanish revolt against Rome, and Spartacus, an ambitious young soldier who becomes a gladiator and eventually leads a rebellion of slaves and hostile minorities, ending his campaign in despair because he has led his followers into disaster. Other Romans, too numerous to mention, complicate the plotlines of the books; many of them are interestingly depicted. Among the non-Romans, mostly rulers, Nicomedes, the elderly king of Bithynia who becomes almost a surrogate grandfather to young Julius Caesar, is a charming and humorous portrait. His fond relationship with his wife, Oradaltis, and their doted upon little dog, amusingly called Sulla, add to Caesar's and the reader's delight in them. Among the women, Aurelia, mother of Julius Caesar and a charming portrait of an ancient working woman, and Julia, wife of Marius and a representation of an ideal Roman matron, are the most significant of many. The gallery of women is much less extensive than that of the men, but the domestic scenes in which they participate are more interesting than the fact-laden descriptions of military campaigns.

ROMAN SOCIETY

A very important aspect of these Roman novels is the depiction of the society. In some ways, the society might almost be considered a character, and McCullough is at pains to portray it fully. Social customs and religious practices are described in detail, even to the extent of the inclusion of a diagram of conventional seating (or, for the men, reclining) at the dinner table. Marriage customs, such as the difference between a conservative version of marriage from which divorce was particularly difficult and less restrictive marital forms, are demonstrated. The debating practices of the Senate are frequently illustrated, as is the manner in which laws were enacted. Technicalities of everyday life—of clothing, of provision for sanitation, of the layout of the streets and buildings of Rome, of the complex system of personal names—are copiously illustrated. Reviewers have noted some anachronisms (allusions to things not possible at that time period), as in McCullough's references to paper and horseshoeing (Tarr 4). Nevertheless, the sense of Roman society and culture is sharp, and the attentive reader, especially the reader who makes use of the glossary and other aids, learns much about life in Rome in the period of the Republic.

Of deeper import than the minutiae of daily life are McCullough's revelations of such aspects of Roman life as the importance of class and ancestry, the position of women, slavery, and the general lack of concern of human life. It is in regards to the depiction of the society that the doubleness of vision so typical of the historical novel becomes especially important. McCullough's readers live in a world in which unthinking brutality and cruelty are considered unacceptable and in which empathy for others is an admirable character trait. Equality of races, sexes, classes is taken for granted as a goal if not as reality. The careless barbarity of the ancient world is shocking today. McCullough's Roman characters would have had no understanding or sympathy for these attitudes. McCullough is at pains to illustrate in a variety of ways how the ancients' value systems, particularly their assumptions about the worth of the individual, differed from those of the present. A man's family background is crucial to his possibilities for any kind of advancement, and the older that family's history is in Rome, the better. Julius Caesar frequently proclaims his descent from the Julii, an old and important family which traces its ancestry back to the goddess Aphrodite. Marius, despite great wealth and ability, is unable to advance because he comes from a non-Roman family, until he allies himself by marriage to the family of the Julii. Sulla, despite his unfortunate beginnings and corruption, is able to advance because he is a member of an old and illustrious family.

Many of the political plots turn on struggles between the various classes, and both Marius and Caesar show their mastery of politics by their abilities to relate to, to understand, and to work with men of classes below their own. Rome's stringently stratified class system is demonstrated to be a cause of much unrest, even leading to civil wars. Class differences which are hard for the contemporary reader to understand underlie much of the political jockeying among characters. Class is based on social and historical origins. The few old families with long histories in Rome, the aristocrats, have great advantages over those whose families have come from outside the city. The possession of wealth, while essential for success, is less crucial than the possession of the correct ancestry. Wealth can be achieved, but nothing can be done about one's birth. Marius and Pompey, outsiders, have initial hurdles that neither Sulla nor Caesar must overcome. As McCullough clearly shows, the social inequities were officially part of the governmental system, each of the higher classes having its own legislative body with powers that changed, as the classes struggled for position. The lower classes lacked political power, and slaves and women of all classes were outside the system. In choosing to live in a poor and ethnically mixed part of Rome, Caesar's mother behaves with striking lack of conventionality and, without intending to do so, gives her son great political advantages. He learns foreign languages and from childhood is accustomed to interacting with people from various countries and social conditions.

The fact that this is a society based on inequality is illustrated in other ways. All families of position have slaves, and it is simply assumed that the losers of a battle or war, if they are not killed, will be sold into slavery. That a human being may be a commodity is an unexamined assumption. The position of women is yet another evidence of the basic inequality of Roman society. Women are seen as commodities, useful in making alliances but of little value in themselves except as sexual objects. They are politically and legally powerless. Some safeguards exist through the dowry system, and if she is divorced a woman generally regains control of her dowry, enabling her to make some kind of life for herself. Before marriage, a woman is totally under the control of her father, and she has no say over whom she will marry unless her father chooses to abide by her wishes, as illustrated in *The First Man in Rome* by the experience of Livia Drusa, married, despite her rebellion, to a man she detests. While she is married, a woman's husband has complete power over her and can divorce her on the whim of the moment, simply by saying so, as Sulla does to Aelia in *The Grass Crown*.

Even more striking evidence of differing attitudes about the worth of human life is given in McCullough's military plots. Battles, sieges of cities, and the aftermaths of military conflicts all illustrate the low value placed on human life and suffering. Or, perhaps, what they illustrate is an inability to empathize with those who are felt to be different or to be enemies. Battle scenes are full of bloodthirstiness and cruelty. The heads of defeated enemies are regularly lopped off and then displayed as evidence of triumph. Torture is acceptable. Crassus, who defeats Spartacus in *Fortune's Favorites*, carries out several particularly horrible examples of military barbarism: decimation and crucifixion. In decimation, a long disused method of punishment for cowardice, Roman soldiers are punished by being lined up in groups of ten, with one from each group chosen by lot. That one is then beaten to death by his nine remaining comrades. Soldiers who have been overrun by Spartacus' mob are punished in this way. Surprisingly, the decimation is successful, for the remaining nine-tenths behave with more courage when tested again. After Spartacus' defeat, his six thousand captured followers are crucified, one every hundred feet, in a line that stretches for miles along the Appian way, as an example for others who might consider rebellion.

One may even joke about crucifying one's future victim, as Caesar, a basically admirable character, does with Polygonus, the pirate captain in *Fortune's Favorites*. And the stoicism with which victims accepted their fates, appearing simply to take them for granted as the way the world worked, is illustrated by Polygonus' joking with Caesar even as he digs the hole into which the cross on which he is to die will be erected.

All these phenomena are of course well attested in the historical record. McCullough has elected to stress them in her interpretation of this portion of the past, and her depiction of the inequality and cruelty of the Roman society is compelling and convincing.

TITLES AND OTHER SYMBOLS

The Romans whom McCullough portrayed in these novels were a people living in an age of omens and premonitions, what we from our vantage point, perhaps rather patronizingly, consider superstition. The predictions of prophetesses and the omens discovered at religious sacrifices and other significant public ceremonies were deeply meaningful to these people. Their actions were often motivated by their beliefs about what was to come, beliefs derived from predictions and auguries. Thus Marius' political career goes forward partly because he is sure that it must, because Martha, the Syrian prophetess, has said it would.

The titles of the novels are of obvious significance, more than simply hinting at the subjects or type of the books. Each of the first three is symbolic, and they become more evocative and less specific in meaning as the series proceeds. *Caesar's Women*, however, bears a purely descriptive title. The opening book in the series, *The First Man in Rome*, obviously refers to Gaius Marius, who becomes what the title of his novel names him and whose career is centered around his striving to achieve and then live up to the prophetess' prediction that he will earn this honor. No less obvious is the symbolism of the title of the second novel, *The Grass Crown,* which initially refers back to the crown the young Julilla idly makes and gives to Sulla and which he takes as a prophecy of what he will accomplish. Thus her act becomes for him just as prophetic as are the words of Martha to Marius. And like the other, Julilla's prediction is fulfilled. Finally, *Fortune's Favorites* is also a meaningful title, reminding readers that Fortune was a deity to the Romans, and so characters in these novels interpret the phrase far more literally than do modern readers. References to both main and secondary characters who are favorites of Fortune run through this novel. Indeed, such references sometimes chart the rising and falling, the successes and failures, of various characters, from Caesar and Pompey (who are still in Fortune's favor at the end of the novel) to Sertorius and Spartacus (who plunge from great success to total defeat).

Occasionally, McCullough makes use of an historical fact symbolically. In *Fortune's Favorites,* a particularly obvious example is the white fawn given to Sertorius by his Spanish followers because they consider it magical and have been impressed by his (to them miraculous) ability to attract animals. He, like them, considers it a symbol of his luck, and when it briefly disappears, he takes that as a terrible omen. When he is assassinated, the fawn is also killed by his assassins and discarded with Sertorius' body like another piece of trash. It had not, after all, brought him luck despite his trust in its magical powers.

McCullough's style in these novels tends to be flat and factual. She makes little use of description for truly evocative purposes. The people she is depicting were, from the twentieth-century perspective, superstitious, and she uses that characteristic to help define and motivate them. The uses of prophecy, of titles, and occasionally of superstitions, then, are among the few occurrences of symbolism.

THEMATIC ISSUES

Thematically, McCullough's Roman novels are rich. Her treatment of the society, the implied comments on its cruelty, its inequality, its classism and sexism and racism are obvious. The mere depiction of these societal characteristics calls them to the attention of the modern reader. They inhere in her materials, in other words. More obviously a result of her choices in interpreting the historical materials are certain other themes. Particularly important among them is the theme of ambition, a trait which has application to the depiction of almost all the important male characters.

Marius, Sulla, Pompey, and Caesar are all ambitious. One of the most important ways in which they are distinguished from each other and their relative goodness or evil is conveyed to the reader is through the nature and expression of that ambition. Marius is personally ambitious, but he is also devoted to his image of Rome. He is patriotic and he acts not from greed or desire to enrich himself—indeed, as a wealthy man he has no need to do so. Nor does he act from desire for power, until near the end of his life when his long struggle with Sulla, his reliance on the prophecy, and perhaps even his continued successes, as well as his bitterly resented defeats, have corrupted him. Thus the angered and embittered man who strikes out at young Caesar, attempting to make it impossible for the boy to outstrip his reputation, is particularly pathetic. In fact, his life, as shown by McCullough, who begins with him as a mature man, is rounded and controlled by the prediction and by the ambition which it feeds and encourages.

Sulla's life is rounded, though not controlled, by his love for Metrobius, his Greek actor lover. The strength of his ambition is revealed by his rejection of Metrobius, with whom he continues to be obsessed until the end of his life. But he puts him aside. His ambition is not disinterested, like Marius but is corrupt from the beginning. He wishes for both power and wealth, but primarily for power. And he uses any means available, including poisoning his stepmother and mistress, to achieve his ends. His extreme cruelty and manipulativeness serve his lust for power. The paradox is that this corrupt man actually does use his seizure of total power, when he becomes Dictator, to enact laws that are, from the conservative point of view, good for Rome, and he yields up his power, restoring the legal government, when he has achieved what he believes must be done.

Two men of the younger generation, Pompey and Caesar, are also ambitious and also contrast with each other. Pompey's ambition, like Sulla's, is personal. He wishes for power and is so arrogant that he frequently misleads himself about his prominence and importance. He repeatedly demands the honors and perquisites he thinks are his due, even when he makes himself the butt of laughter for so doing. He is defeated his first time in battle, perhaps because of his very certainty that he cannot be beaten. As he returns home from Spain near the end of *For-*

tune's Favorites, a characteristic passage, told from his viewpoint, indicates how his ambition and pride mislead him:

> He was, he knew, undoubtedly the First Man in Rome. But he also knew that no one who mattered would ever admit the fact. So he would have to prove it to everyone, and the only way he could do that was to bring off some coup so staggering in its audacity and so glaringly unconstitutional that after it was done all men would *have* to accord him his rightful title of the First Man in Rome. (723)

The arrogance of his applying to himself the title Marius had won so gloriously a generation earlier is of a piece with his having given himself the nickname "Magnus" while still an untested youngster. His ambition and its accompanying confidence are extreme.

Caesar, no less ambitious and no less confident than Pompey, is both cleverer and more patient. His confidence is always merited, unlike Pompey's and unlike Pompey's it does not express itself in demands for rewards and recognition. He is willing to forego these in order to build a base for long-term success. In a passage which parallels thematically that of Pompey quoted above, Caesar tells a superior,

> "The pattern of my life is set. I will get nothing as a favor and much against bitter opposition. I stand above the rest and I will outdo the rest. But never, I swear, unconstitutionally. I will make my way up the *cursus honorum* exactly as the law prescribes." (*Fortune's Favorites* 656)

The contrast between Pompey's willingness to flout the law and Caesar's insistence on abiding by it is obvious. Each is ambitious, but only Caesar is willing to temper his ambition by any scruples.

Other themes are of course obvious in these long and complex narratives. The lust for power, complexities of political rivalry, greed and financial corruption, even military tactics might also be considered significant themes. All are explored from novel to novel as the series proceeds. This series differs, in fact, from McCullough's other novels in the large number of themes, all of them inherent in the historical materials, which are examined. This very wealth of themes, lacking focus on one or two as central, is one of the problems of the books. There is so much here that the reader has trouble keeping it all in mind, and it is not sorted out by the author. The theme of ambition is an exception in being handled with some subtlety, and it comes closer than do any of the others to unifying the novels so far published.

A FEMINIST READING OF "THE MASTERS OF ROME" SERIES

As we saw earlier (see the fuller discussion in the feminist reading of *The Thorn Birds*), feminism is a social movement with important implications for literary criticism. Feminist literary interpretations often concentrate on examining the portrayals of female characters, the examinations of women's issues, and the general attitudes towards women revealed in a piece of literature. In McCullough's fiction generally, female characters tend to be the most interesting, but they typically have difficult lives. This is particularly true of the women in the Roman novels, where, though the female characters are among the most interesting and believable, they are also minor or fringe characters. They play only indirect roles in the political plots and no roles at all in the military plots. They are relegated to the personal plots, where they are indeed often very important. But the personal lives of the male characters are of less importance to them than their public lives, which effectively indicates how unimportant women were in that time.

Wives are replaceable. Divorce is easy. Sulla divorces a blameless wife, in *The Grass Crown,* because he finds her boring. His decision to do so is triggered simply by an idle remark she makes, and his pretext is that she is childless. When she is devastated by his sudden action, he behaves with total lack of concern for her feelings. Marius is only a little kinder to his first wife. When Julia's father, poor but aristocratic, approaches him in *The First Man in Rome,* suggesting that they could help each other if Julia marries Marius, he points out that he is already married but that is no real impediment. Marius divorces his wife almost as easily as Sulla does later. Marius, at least, shows some concern for the financial well-being of his discarded spouse, but the cruelty of the system and the helplessness of the women are equally evident. The difference between these two, at first collaborators and then bitter rivals, is revealed by their behaviors towards the women they cast off as hindrances.

Girls are the powerless subjects of their fathers until they marry. The experience of Livia Drusa, engaged by her father to a man she hates in

The First Man in Rome, is a striking example. When she refuses to obey, she is imprisoned in the family home until finally she agrees. Marriages are arranged, as the experience of Julia and Livia shows, to suit the political needs of the fathers; the young women's own inclinations are unimportant. Julia's father does consult her, unlike Livia's, and she is fortunate that her marriage is a happy one. That Livia's marriage is not happy matters to no one except herself. Fathers are pleased by the birth of girl babies, because those daughters will give them bargaining chips to be used in cementing power relationships. For that reason, Caesar rejoices at the birth of his daughter in *Fortune's Favorites.* He thinks ahead to her later potential usefulness. Marriages can occur at various ages, since the principal consideration is the union of families, not the happiness of individuals. Cinnilla is a child when she marries Caesar, and their marriage cannot be consummated for many years. Julia is a teenager when she marries the middle-aged Marius. But in each case, the age of the young wife is less important than the political advantage she brings to her husband. Since the women are well-drawn characters, with their often hopeless yearnings and thwarted feelings touchingly portrayed, the injustice of a system which reduces them to objects, to political bargaining chips, is vividly presented. McCullough does, however, show the protection which is given to the women by the dowry system. In the event of widowhood or divorce, a woman would have a degree of financial security, though her husband usually had the use of her money during their marriage.

McCullough often uses their attitudes towards women, particularly their wives, to characterize important male characters. Several times she employs the technique of revealing something about a marital or sexual relationship as she introduces an important character. For example, *Fortune's Favorites* opens with Pompey in bed with his young wife. Her infatuation with him is obvious, but his view of her as completely expendable is almost immediately clear. Sulla cynically uses his stepmother and mistress both financially and sexually and then murders them when they are in his way. Marius unemotionally casts off his first wife (though he does provide for her financial future), but he is a good and loving husband to Julia. Caesar is a good son and a kind and loving husband to his child bride. He is also, however, a womanizer, taking pleasure in seducing the wives of prominent men. In each case, these behaviors towards women mirror their behaviors in other areas of life. Even a relatively briefly depicted character like Spartacus reveals his character partly by his relationship with a woman. The female slave who helps him achieve his escape becomes his consort, and their relationship is one of loving equals. King Nicomedes, an elderly eastern ruler who befriends Caesar, shows his humanity by his affectionate relationship with his wife Oradaltis—and even with their little dog.

The two principal female characters, who are woven through the personal plots of *The First Man in Rome, The Grass Crown,* and *Fortune's Favorites,* are Julia, Marius' wife, and Aurelia, Caesar's mother. Julia is an example of a wisely maternal and wifely woman. Knowing that Marius is much older than she and that their marriage is an unconventional one, she yet agrees to it with pleasure. As wife and mother she is above reproach. She serves as a model of the perfect Roman matron, supportive of her husband and nurturing of her child, young Marius, and her nephew Caesar. At her death, the last of her family for she outlives both husband and son, her funeral is a symbolic closing of an era, allowing Rome finally to mourn for Marius, who had died under a shadow. A likable character, she fits well into her society, meeting its expectations and living a fulfilling life.

A more complex character is Aurelia. Married to Gaius Julius Caesar, who she knows will be off on military business much of the time, she makes the unconventional choice of investing her dowry in an apartment house in a disreputable portion of the city. The ground floor is reserved for Aurelia and her family, while the upper stories are rented out to a motley collection of poor families of various nationalities. Eventually she is able to take the still more unconventional step of becoming her own apartment manager, and thus she becomes a working woman. And she is a very good one, able to relate well to a variety of people and wise in her control of her property. She provides an environment that is of great help to her son, for he learns languages from her polyglot tenants and discovers how to get along with all kinds of people, neither acting superior nor patronizing them. However, as a mother she is less completely satisfactory, for having to be both mother and father to Caesar, she does not show him the affection he craves. For that, he turns to his aunt Julia, the more purely domestic woman. It is a tribute to McCullough's use of her historical materials that her portrayal of Aurelia as working woman is completely believable and in no way feels anachronistic.

There are a number of other brief portraits of women in these novels, and some of those characters come vividly to life. But they all emphasize the subordinate position of women in this very unequal society. Some are shallow and flighty, like Julilla, Julia's sister and Sulla's first wife, illustrating what may become of women who have no purpose other than to be pawns in the power struggles of their fathers, sexual partners to their husbands, and mothers to their children. Some men do share their lives with their women, and those men are the most admirable. Marius, Caesar, Spartacus, even King Nicomedes are shown to be human and likable by the very fact that they respect and like their women.

When Julia is dying, Aurelia sums up the pathos of the situation of these women. Pointing out that Julia has no longer any reason to live, for both her husband and son are dead, she says, "A woman's life is in her men. . . . No woman truly esteems her lot, it is thankless and obscure. Men move and control the world, not women. So the intelligent woman lives her life through her men" (*Fortune's Favorites* 790). These words, from the most independent and successful of the women in these novels, summarize the low position of the Roman woman.

For feminist readers, these novels present a dark picture of the past. Women were legally powerless, totally dependent on the goodwill and kindness of first their fathers, then their husbands, and finally their sons. But despite these handicaps, some women did manage to carve out rich and fulfilling lives. Julia and Aurelia are the most prominent examples, but there are other strong women. Among them are Spartacus' lover and Livia Drusa, who grows from a giddy girl with a crush on a neighbor whose name she doesn't even know, through an unhappy forced marriage to brief fulfillment in a loving marriage. Shallow and weak women who cannot cope with their situations are also present. Julilla, Julia's sister and Sulla's first wife, is one example. The gallery of women is large and varied.

The fourth novel, published shortly before this book went to press, in "The Masters of Rome" series, entitled *Caesar's Women*, continues the general patterns of development of the preceding books, though political and especially personal plot lines are given more emphasis than the military events. Focus, to a degree, is shifted from the male figures so stressed earlier to women characters. As the title indicates, Julius Caesar remains central, and such familiar characters as Aurelia, now an old woman, and Pompey continue, alongside many new personages.

As McCullough points out in the "Author's Note" which follows the text of the novel, with this book she has reached a period in Roman history when there are many more sources and therefore much more precise knowledge about historical personages, including women, than for earlier years. *Caesar's Women* covers the decade from June in the year 68 B.C. to March of 58 B.C. McCullough defends her "novelization of history" explicitly in her afterword, reemphasizing the thoroughness of her research. The historical novel, considered "as a technique of historical exploration and deduction," she says, "has something to recommend it—provided that the writer is thoroughly steeped in the history of the period concerned." Summarizing her method, she says, "I work in the correct way, from the ancient sources to the modern scholars, and I make up my own mind from my own work whilst not dismissing opinion and advice from modern Academe," and she indicates that her continuing research has made her unhappy with some (unspecified) aspects of the earlier books (635).

Readers who have found the personal and political aspects of the Roman novels particularly interesting will be especially pleased to have this fourth novel available, as will those who are more comfortable with the more familiar subject matter of the later period. Those who found the earlier books especially valuable because they provided an introduction to lesser known historical materials may, however, find *Caesar's Women* less informative. The fifth novel in the series, it is announced here, will likely be titled *Let the Dice Fly*.

Bibliography

WORKS BY COLLEEN McCULLOUGH

Caesar's Women. New York: William Morrow and Company, 1996.
Creed for the Third Millennium, A. 1985. New York: Avon, 1986.
First Man in Rome, The. New York: William Morrow and Company, 1990.
Fortune's Favorites. New York: William Morrow and Company, 1993.
Grass Crown, The. New York: William Morrow and Company, 1991.
Indecent Obsession, An. 1981. New York: Avon, 1982.
Ladies of Missalonghi, The. New York: Harper & Row, 1987.
Thorn Birds, The. New York: Harper & Row, 1977.
Tim. 1974. New York: Avon, 1990.

WORKS ABOUT COLLEEN McCULLOUGH

General Information and Criticism about Colleen McCullough

Cassill, Kay. "The Thorned Words of Colleen McCullough." *Writer's Digest* March 1980: 32, 34–36.
McDowell, Edwin. "Behind the Best Sellers: Colleen McCullough." *New York Times Book Review* 15 November 1981: 42.
Rovner, Sandy. "Colleen McCullough in Paradise: Down Under & Laughing All the Way to the Top." Washington *Post* 26 November 1981: C1, C23.

Steinberg, Sybil. "Colleen McCullough: The Indefatigable Australian Author Has Embarked on a Five-volume Series Set in Ancient Rome." *Publishers Weekly* 14 September 1990: 109–10.

Toomey, Philippa. "Nurse McCullough Dispenses a Second Best-Seller." *Times* (London) 30 November 1981: 8.

Biographical Information about Colleen McCullough

Dougherty, Paul. "*Thorn Birds* Author Colleen McCullough Finds Love in the Outback with a Housepainter Husband." *People Weekly* 7 May 1984: 135.

Feldman, Gayle. "Sparks Fly as Colleen McCullough Leaves Harper for Hearst." *Publishers Weekly* 21 July 1989: 40.

"McCullough, Colleen." *Contemporary Authors* (New Revision Series). New York: Gale Research Inc., 1995, 46: 263–66.

Reuter, Madalynne. "Avon Buys 'The Thorn Birds' for Record $1.9-Million." *Publishers Weekly* 7 March 1977: 27–28.

REVIEWS AND CRITICISM

Tim

Canby, Vincent. "Film: 'Tim,' a Romantic Drama from Australia." *New York Times* 17 September 1981: C25.

Ferrari, Margaret. "Tim." *America* 10 August 1974: 59–60.

Scott, R. E. "McCullough, Colleen. *Tim*." *Library Journal* 1 April 1974: 1059.

The Thorn Birds

Breslin, John B. "*GWTW* Down Under, and 'All God's Plenty.' " *America* 21 May 1977: 468–69.

Bridgwood, Christine. "Family Romances: The Contemporary Popular Family Saga." In *The Progress of Romance: The Politics of Popular Fiction*. Jean Radford, ed. London: Routledge & Kegan Paul, 1986. 167–93.

Brookner, Anita. "Continental Drift." *TLS* 7 October 1977: 1135.

Caplan, Pat. "Everyone's Nice, Life Goes On—A Page-Turner?" *The National Observer* 20 June 1977: 18.

Clemons, Walter. "Bed of Thorns." *Newsweek* 25 April 1977: 93, 96, 99.

de Usabel, Frances Esmonde. "McCullough, Colleen. The Thorn Birds." *Library Journal* 1 May 1977: 1044.

Fremont-Smith, Eliot. "True Grit Pays Off." *The Village Voice* 28 March 1977: 93.

Gray, Paul. "Shaking the Money Tree." *Time* 9 May 1977: 85.

Heller, Amanda. "The Thorn Birds." *Atlantic Monthly* June 1977: 91.

Kaplan, Cora. "The Thorn Birds: Fiction, Fantasy, Feminity." In *Formations of Fantasy.* Victor Burgin and others, eds. London: Methuen, 1986. 142–66.

Kroll, Steven. *"The Thorn Birds." Commonweal* 22 July 1977: 473–75.

Lehmann-Haupt, Christopher. "The Song Is Familiar." New York *Times* 2 May 1977: 31.

Mathewson, Ruth. "Putting Down 'The Thorn Birds.' " *The New Leader* 4 July 1977: 15–16.

Morris, Gwen. "An Australian Ingredient in American Soap: *The Thorn Birds* by Colleen McCullough." *Journal of Popular Culture* 24: 4 (Spring 1991): 59–69.

Murray, James G. "The Thorn Birds." *The Critic* 35 (Summer 1977): 72–74.

O'Connor, John J. "TV View: Strong Performances Help 'Thorn Birds' Soar." *New York Times* 27 March 1983: H31.

Parasuram, Laxmi. *"The Thorn Birds:* An Australian Odyssey." *Journal of Australian Literature* 1: 1 (1990) 101–10.

Prial, Frank J. " 'Thorn Birds' [television miniseries] Begins Sunday, Despite Religious Objections." *New York Times* 26 March 1983: 48.

Schott, Webster. "Golden Fleece." *New York Review of Books* 8 May 1977: 13, 18, 20.

Shales, Tom. "Sheep, Sin and Celibacy in the Wilds of Australia." Rev. of television miniseries. Washington *Post* 27 March 1983: K1, K4–5.

Turner, Alice K. "Cardinal Sin." Washington *Post* 24 April 1977: E1–2.

Udosen, Willye Bell. "Names and Symbols of Characters in *The Thorn Birds.*" *Papers of the North Central Names Institute.* Vol. 4. DeKalb: Illinois Name Society, 1984. 43–65.

An Indecent Obsession

Greenberg, Joanne. "Love and Duty." *New York Times Book Review* 25 October 1981: 14, 54.

Grimstad, Kirsten. "A Microuniverse in a Mental Ward." Los Angeles *Times Book Review* 25 October 1981: 12–13.

Helm, Thomas E. Rev. in *The Christian Century* 31 March 1982: 383–84.

Lehmann-Haupt, Christopher. "Books of The Times." *New York Times* 29 October 1981: C24.

Rumens, Carol. "Within the Starched Breast." *TLS* 11 December 1981: 1448.

A Creed for the Third Millennium

Gray, Paul. "Mental Paste." *Time* 20 May 1985: 80–81.
Mitchell, Lisa. "A Creed for the Third Millennium." Los Angeles *Times Book Review* 21 July 1985: 6.

The Ladies of Missalonghi

Anderson, Peter. "Part Three: Don Quixote on Wall Street." *Meanjin* (Australia) 48: 2 (Winter 1989): 284–90.
"Ladies of Missalonghi, The." Rev. in Los Angeles *Times Book Review* 21 June 1987: 4.
"Ladies of Missalonghi, The." Rev. in *Publishers Weekly* 20 February 1987: 73.
Saunders, David. "Part Two: The Work and Its Double: Literary Resemblances and the Law." *Meanjin* (Australia) 48: 2 (Winter 1989): 276–83.
Whitlock, Gillian. "Double Trouble: Part One. One or Two Women?" *Meanjin* (Australia) 48: 2 (Winter 1989): 269–75.
Yolen, Jane. "Vacant Lives in Great Big Australia." *New York Times Book Review* 26 April 1987: 15.

"The Masters of Rome" Series

Buck, Mason. "When in Rome: Fortune's Favorites." *New York Times Book Review* 24 October 1993: 22.
Campbell, Don G. "McCullough's Roman à Clef: The First Man in Rome." Los Angeles *Times Book Review* 28 October 1990: 11.
"First Man in Rome, The." Rev. in *Time* 15 October 1990: 88.
"Fortune's Favorites." Rev. in *Publishers Weekly* 23 October 1993: 58.
"Grass Crown, The." Rev. in *Publishers Weekly* 9 August 1991: 43.
Jennings, Gary. "Roman Scandals: The Grass Crown." *New York Times Book Review* 6 October 1991: 13.
McCullough, Colleen. "Reflections upon Her Long Historical Novels." Unpub. essay, distributed by William Morrow and Company upon publication of *Fortune's Favorites.*
Rinzler, Carol E. "Roman Soap: The First Man in Rome." *New York Times Book Review* 4 November 1990: 19.
Seaman, Donna. "McCullough, Colleen. Fortune's Favorites." *Booklist* 1 September 1993: 5.

Sussman, Steven. "McCullough, Colleen. Fortune's Favorites." *Library Journal* 1 September 1993: 222.

Tarr, Judith. "On the Way to the Forum: Fortune's Favorites." *Book World* 21 November 1993: 4.

OTHER SECONDARY SOURCES

Cawelti, John G. *Adventure, Mystery, and Romance: Formula Stories as Art and Popular Culture.* Chicago: Chicago UP, 1976.

Christian-Smith, Linda K. *Becoming a Woman through Romance.* New York: Routledge, 1990.

Montgomery, L. M. *The Blue Castle.* 1926. Canada: McClelland and Stewart, 1972.

Index

About the Author

MARY JEAN DeMARR is the Professor Emerita of English and Women's Studies at Indiana State University. She is co-author, with Jane S. Bakerman, of two books, *Adolescent Female Portraits in the American Novel, 1961–1981: An Annotated Bibliography* (1983) and *The Adolescent in the American Novel Since 1960* (1986). She is editor of *In the Beginning: First Novels in Mystery Series* (1995) and co-editor of *The Dog Didn't Do It: Animals in Mysteries* (forthcoming). Her major interests are modern American literature, women's literature, and detective and other popular fiction.